STEPFAMILIES OF THE BIBLE

Timeless Wisdom for Blended Families

LAURA PETHERBRIDGE

Stepfamilies of the Bible: Timeless Wisdom for Blended Families
Copyright © 2025 by Laura Petherbridge

Published in association with Story Architect. www.booksandsuch.com

All rights reserved. No part of this publication may be reproduced, stored in a retrieval system, or transmitted in any form or by any means—electronic, mechanical, photocopy, recording or any other—except for brief quotations in printed reviews without the written prior permission of the publisher.

The website addresses recommended throughout this book are offered as a resource to you. These websites are not intended in any way to be or imply an endorsement on the part of Story Architect, nor do we vouch for their content.

Details in some stories have been changed to protect the identities of the persons involved.

No AI Training. Any use of this publication to "train" artificial intelligence (AI) technologies to generate text is expressly prohibited.

Unless otherwise noted, Scripture quotations are taken from the Holy Bible, New International Version®, NIV®. Copyright © 1973, 1978, 1984, 2011 by Biblica, Inc.® Used by permission of Zondervan. All rights reserved worldwide. www.zondervan.com The "NIV" and "New International Version" are trademarks registered in the United States Patent and Trademark Office by Biblica, Inc.® Scripture quotations marked (NLT) are taken from the *Holy Bible*, New Living Translation, copyright ©1996, 2004, 2015 by Tyndale House Foundation. Used by permission of Tyndale House Publishers, Carol Stream, Illinois 60188. All rights reserved. Scripture quotations marked HCSB are taken from the Holman Christian Standard Bible®, Copyright © 1999, 2000, 2002, 2003, 2009 by Holman Bible Publishers. Used by permission. Holman Christian Standard Bible®, Holman CSB®, and HCSB® are federally registered trademarks of Holman Bible Publishers. Scripture quotations are from the ESV® Bible (The Holy Bible, English Standard Version®), © 2001 by Crossway, a publishing ministry of Good News Publishers. Used by permission. All rights reserved. The ESV text may not be quoted in any publication made available to the public by a Creative Commons license. The ESV may not be translated in whole or in part into any other language.

Book Cover by Hannah Linder Designs

Edited by Criss Bertling

Print ISBN: 978-1-962845-21-2

Printed in the United States of America

Contents

Foreword ································· xi
Introduction: Stepfamilies of the Bible - Really? ······ xv

1. Overcoming Jealousy and Resentment:
   Abraham, Sarah, and Hagar ················ 1
2. Overcoming Rejection:
   Laban, Jacob, Rebekah, and Leah ············ 31
3. Overcoming Despair:
   Elkanah, Hannah, and Peninnah ············ 49
4. Overcoming Bitterness: Joseph Part 1 -
   Siblings, Stepsiblings, and Half-Siblings ······· 61
5. Overcoming Resentment, Finding Forgiveness:
   Joseph Part 2 - When Your Family Hurts You ···· 77
6. Overcoming Shame: King David Part 1 –
   Wives, Wives, and More Wives ·············· 95
7. Overcoming Failure: King David Part 2 –
   Poor Choices ·························· 117
8. Overcoming Insults: Jesus and His Half-Siblings ··· 135
9. Biological Family vs. Blended Family:
   Digging Deeper into the Differences ········· 153
10. Adding an "Ours" Baby ···················· 171
11. Stepfamily Steps to Victory ················· 183

Appendix: For Moms and Stepmoms ·············· 193
More Resources ····························· 203

Foreword

God's people have always included families with complex configurations, intricate dynamics, and storylines you'd rather not repeat in front of young children. Specifically, stepfamilies are nothing new. They are as old as the early characters of the Bible. But even seminary-trained leaders look at you funny when you point out the obvious. For over thirty years now I've chuckled at the faces of pastors when I speak about the dysfunction of Abraham's not-so-blended family, Jacob's four-wife stepfamily, David's generationally sexually disgraceful household, or the fact that Jesus had a stepfather. *What?* their faces say. *I never thought of it like that before.* It's all there. It's always been there. (We just didn't see it—or didn't want to see it). But that's what should give us pause to hope. The fact that complex, imperfect families have always been part of God's people is good news! It reminds us that we, too—as imperfect and in need of grace as we are—are welcome in His house.

And there's something else. If family structure doesn't make or break your ability to walk with God, then what should we focus on? It's what comes from inside a man, Jesus says in Mark 7:20-23, that determines sin or righteousness, not what begins outside him. All of the central qualities that build godliness and contribute to healthy relationships flow from the heart, not the structure of the home. Blended families can laugh like biological families, they can learn from their mistakes like the unmarried, repent from selfish choices like a widow, grow in their ability to walk in the way of Christ like a childless adult, and can live holy and dedicated lives to the Lord like a newly married couple. Just like everyone else, they can act in ways that could be described as love, joy, peace, patience, kindness, goodness, faithfulness, gentleness, and self-control, and they can contribute to God's Kingdom agenda for the world.

Now, having said that, the relational structure of a home does lend itself to advantageous and disadvantageous. Homes that begin with two committed believers who covenant with one another till death do them part, who then have children together and raise them in the fear and admonition of the Lord, have relational advantages and find it easier to pursue the goals they have in raising their children and loving one another. But it's still the heart of each person that determines whether that goal will be reached. On the other hand, single-parent homes and blended families do face disadvantages that other families do not. Unique dynamics make living, loving, and trusting one another more difficult. But most of the time, the challenges are not insurmountable, especially with the careful application of God's word supported by practical wisdom arriving from the study of stepfamily dynamics.

In this book, *Stepfamilies of the Bible,* Laura Petherbridge contributes yet another work designed to do just that—shed light on God's design for the heart and the home and offer blended families practical insights for building a loving and safe family. Her primary narrative is the Bible itself and the stories we know so well. Or, *thought* we knew so well.

As you read, see if you didn't experience what I did. When you really dig, there's more to these people than perhaps we first thought. There's more to their story, more depth to their character. And when you jump inside their complex world and sit for a while, they...well, they become more human. Their odd decisions become sort of understandable. Their feelings and fears seem strangely familiar to my own. And the journey they walk with God, much the same as ours.

The stepfamilies of the Bible are people. They are us and we are them.

Go now on a journey with them to better see yourself. Look past the structure of their home (and your inclination to judge) to their qualities worth emulating, their mistakes worth avoiding, and their faith worth repeating.

> — Ron Deal, blended family author,
> speaker, and therapist
> www.SmartStepfamilies.com

Introduction: Stepfamilies of the Bible - Really?

It has taken me six years to write this book, whereas my other books took nine to twelve months. I'd start writing for two to three months and then wonder if people would want to read it or publishers would want to print it. I'd become discouraged, disorganized, or confused and stop writing.

However, whenever I tried to start a new project, I felt God nudging me back to this one. I needed to get over my chaotic feelings and write the book.

The timeless stepfamilies of old illuminate God's truth with their wise and wicked choices. The antiquated is applicable. The relic becomes relevant. Looking back on these stepfamilies, aka blended families, can provide in-depth awareness, wisdom, and solutions for current complexities.

Perhaps the greatest treasure biblical blended families provide is the insight into overcoming when life gets problematic and wearisome. A strong, unified marriage can be formed by the couple who discovers how to triumph over the day-to-day stressors and complexities.

In the Old Testament, there are times when God appears cruel and heartless. It's not true, but it is hard to comprehend. We grapple with the age-old question of why a loving God would allow such things to happen. As a person's journey with God grows and strengthens, we discover that His ways are often a mystery. It's natural to ask, "Why?" However, when no suitable answer arrives, and we wallow in the unknown, we can discover how to embrace His trustworthy goodness and holiness. Maturity in Christ brings acceptance and trust in God's authority. And because He's a good, wise Almighty Father—the ultimate parent—He allows our Bible brothers and sisters to experience the consequence of a poor choice when they persist in disobedience and unrepentance. God is not an enabler. He knows the perfect how and when to say—NO!

God doesn't owe me an explanation for His why.

God doesn't change.

Reading the Old Testament can sometimes feel like watching a movie with multiple characters, plots, and storylines. We encounter patriarchs, delinquents, heroes, bullies, the sanctified and the slaves, the prominent and the prisoners. In one situation, the Bible might share a great deal about the person; in the next, we get merely a snippet. God has preserved the narratives of these remarkable Old Testament families—hideous and holy—to teach us how to form, nurture, and sustain a godly blended family.

Our Creator's holy character shines brightly as He advises and chastises these precious stepfamilies. Perhaps, more than in any other circumstances, we see God as the same, "yesterday, today and forever" (Hebrews 13:8).

I love this quote from Abraham Joshua Heschel.

> *The omnipotence of God is not always perceptible, but the omnipotence of the Bible is the great miracle of history. Like God, it is often misused and distorted by unclean minds,*

yet its capacity to withstand the most vicious attacks is boundless. The vigor and veracity of its ideas are perceptible under the rust and batter of two millennia of debate and dogma: it does not fade in spite of theology nor collapse under abuse. The Bible is the perpetual motion of the spirit, an ocean of meaning, its waves beating against man's abrupt and steep shortcomings, its echo reaching into the blind alleys of his wrestling with despair.

No sadder proof can be given by a man of his own spiritual opacity than his insensitiveness to the Bible. A ship that looms large in the river seems tiny when on the ocean. "The greatness of the Bible becomes more manifest when studied within the framework of universal history, and its majesty increases with the reader's familiarity.

Irrefutably, indestructibly, never wearied by time, the Bible wanders through the ages, giving itself with ease to all men, as if it belonged to every soul on earth. It speaks in every language and in every age. It benefits all the arts and does not compete with them. We all draw upon it, and it remains pure, inexhaustible, and complete. In three thousand years it has not aged a day. It is a book that cannot die. Oblivion shuns its pages. Its power is not subsiding. In fact, it is still at the very beginning of its career, the full meaning of its content having hardly touched the threshold of our minds; *like an ocean at the bottom of which countless pearls lie, waiting to be discovered, its spirit is still to be unfolded. Though its words seem plain and its idiom translucent, unnoticed meanings, undreamed-of intimations break forth constantly. More than two thousand years of reading and research have not succeeded in exploring its full meaning. Today it is as if it had never been touched, never been seen, as if we had not even begun to read it.*

Its spirit is too much for one generation to bear. Its words reveal more than we can absorb. All we usually accomplish is the attempt to appropriate a few single lines so that our spirit becomes synonymous with a passage.[1]

Precious to God

All flesh is grass,
  And all the goodliness thereof is as the flower of the field…
  The grass withers, the flower fades,
  But the word of our God shall stand for ever. Isaiah 40:6-8

Before we dive in, it's necessary to explain something our current culture doesn't fully understand. It's not addressed in every church or modern society. However, it is a subject that must be acknowledged if we desire to embrace the grace and mercy God shows to every person and stepfamily. It is the subject of sin.

What is sin? The dictionary says:

Sin is

- an offense against religious or moral law
- an action that is or is felt to be highly reprehensible
- a serious shortcoming
- transgression of the law of God
- a vitiated state of human nature in which the self is estranged from God[2]

In its simplest explanation, it's man's rebellion against God. It's the human desire to be God. It's the entire reason why Jesus came to earth. Christians believe that Jesus was

---

[1] Lifeway Press, 2024, Brentwood, TN, Kristi McLelland, video clip spoken

[2] https://www.merriam-webster.com/dictionary

born for the purpose of paying the price for our sins. We believe His death and resurrection heal the gap between God and man. When we confess our sins and believe that Jesus Christ paid the price for our sins on the cross, and we ask God to forgive us, we can be fully restored into perfect fellowship with Him.

> *But if we walk in the light, as he is in the light, we have fellowship with one another, and the blood of Jesus, his Son, purifies us from all sin. If we claim to be without sin, we deceive ourselves and the truth is not in us. If we confess our sins, he is faithful and just and will forgive us our sins and purify us from all unrighteousness.* 1 John 1:7-9

You may be married to a person who has no desire for God's help with stepfamily living. Don't be discouraged. This resource can assist and influence your entire family. Concentrate on the areas you control and allow the Holy Spirit to guide your spouse.

I have used the phrases stepfamily and blended family interchangeably in this book. These two phrases refer to any person who is dating, engaged, or married to someone who has children from a previous relationship.

Join me in the journey of identifying, appreciating, and embracing the *Stepfamilies of the Bible*.

~ 1 ~
Overcoming Jealousy and Resentment
Abraham, Sarah, and Hagar

"Open to Genesis chapter one."

My friend Barb and I obediently began riffling through the thick pages of our brand-new, stiff Bibles. Neither of us had a clue where to find Genesis. Oh, yes, we tried. But when we couldn't, we just looked at each other, hoping no one would notice, especially the women's Bible study leader.

"Page one," the kind lady seated to my right whispered.

"Thanks," I meekly replied.

It was painfully obvious neither of us had ever opened a Bible. But this day would change my life. It opened a door in my mind to an entirely new and spectacular world I never knew existed: the Holy Bible and its love letters from God to His people, written by the hands of His people.

I was 24 years old and passionate about attending my first Bible study. Barb and I met while joining Mary Kay Cosmetics as beauty consultants. As a "baby Christian," I was exceedingly enthusiastic to share my faith with her. She didn't want to hear about it. But I eventually persuaded

Barb to attend my church by coaxing her with the lure (sometimes known as coercion) of hearing a "great motivational speaker" – my pastor. She reluctantly agreed. The next Sunday, she joined me again. As the service was ending, the pastor asked if anyone wanted to give their life to Christ. Barb got up from her seat and walked the aisle to the altar. I was stunned and ecstatic. This should be proof positive that God can use anyone for His kingdom and that it is His truth that draws people to Himself.

We were baby Christians together. Oblivious to anything holy, our hearts were hungry for truth, and our minds—like sponges—soaked up His words. That was in 1981.

Barb and I now live miles apart; however, our friendship remains strong. We both love sharing the memory of that first day of Bible study. We sometimes embellish the story with colorful illustrations of how gorgeous we were decked out in our perfectly coiffed outfits, donning our bright Mary Kay pins. We laugh hilariously as we reminisce about our naïve, adolescent approach to Bible study. But God saw us. He still sees us. And I suspect He probably laughed at our big, puffy, 80s hairstyles.

I know we do.

It's a wonderful illustration and reminder of how to approach this resource.

Do not be discouraged or intimidated if you are new to the Bible. Even to those who have studied Scripture for a long time, the Old Testament can seem daunting. Go slowly. Learn from ancient saints and sinners. Embrace and appreciate these multiple and multifaceted families. Take the time to read and re-read each scenario carefully.

Remember, any person who is a follower of Christ has the Holy Spirit living within him/her. Part of His role is to guide and teach us in God's integrity and loyalty. If we ask, He provides insight and correction for any misinterpretation of God's Holy Word. Look to Him for revelation regarding the Scriptures, especially when they seem confusing, or the culture of the Old Testament doesn't make sense. The more you read the Bible under the guidance of the Holy Spirit, the easier it becomes to understand.

God's book isn't like other books. His words are alive, razor-sharp, and the breath of life. His teaching can produce a fresh wind and immaculate wisdom to anyone who asks.

For the word of God is alive and active. Sharper than any double-edged sword, it penetrates even to dividing soul and spirit, joints, and marrow; it judges the thoughts and attitudes of the heart. Hebrews 4:12

As we apply the teachings, compassion, and insights from God's stepfamilies, keep in mind that God is eager to reveal a new thing, a better way, and undying hope - if we humbly ask.

For those new to Christianity or who may be uncertain of who God is, my hope is that you discover the One who is waiting for you with open arms. God eagerly embraces anyone who desires truth and never shuns, abandons, or shames those who are sincerely hungry to learn about Him. If at any point you feel confused or upset while reading, just pause. Get quiet and whisper this prayer: "God, I want to know you. I need you to help me understand. Teach me what you want me to know."

If you have never asked Jesus Christ into your life, there's no better time than right now. Perhaps you have attended church your entire life, but this insight about God seems foreign to you. It's perfectly okay. In fact—it's fabulous. God is thrilled to have you explore his words and teachings. So am I.

Let us begin to discover God's blended families who lived long ago.

Humans are Human

"I'm so tired of the fighting between my home, my kids, and my ex-wife," Jeff sighed.

"I'm in a no-win situation. No matter what I do, someone will be mad at me," he continued.

"There is no 'right' answer because both sides have a valid point. I'm in the middle of a hostile war that forces me to choose between my wife and my kids. If I pick my wife, my ex tells the kids, 'See, your dad loves his new wife more than he does you.' If I side with my kids, my spouse says, 'I'm your spouse. You're disrespecting me. You should be siding with me.' The friction is killing me, and I'm at a total loss. Will this battle between the two homes ever end?"

Stepfamilies everywhere are nodding in agreement saying, "Yep! Change a few names, and that's our house." There is consolation in knowing it's normal. But the sentiment typically doesn't last for long and doesn't bring a solution.

What may offer some reassurance is to delve into the first book of the Bible.

Starting in Genesis 12, we read about the life of the amazing patriarch, Abraham (he begins as Abram and God changes his name). I will use Abraham (and his wife Sarah) as their names throughout the chapter. This is God's guy, specifically chosen for a huge task that would affect all of mankind until this present day. It's fascinating to note that Abraham was not raised in a godly home; his ancestors worshiped various gods.

> *And Joshua said to all the people, "Thus says the Lord, the God of Israel, 'Long ago, your fathers lived beyond the Euphrates, Terah, the father of Abraham and of Nahor; and they served other gods."* Joshua 24:2

This should be a tremendous encouragement for those like me who were not raised in a Christian home. God chooses whom He chooses. God looks at the heart, not the DNA. Because God knows everything about us, He knows who is right for a job and who isn't. Sometimes, we don't understand His choices or ways, but He can be trusted.

Abraham's seed is the basis for three of the world's major religions. In Judaism, the promised offspring is from Abraham's son, Isaac, born of his wife Sarah, which forms the religion of Judaism. The genealogy of Jesus is Isaac, which is the foundation for Christianity. Abraham's firstborn son, Ishmael, born of Hagar, led to the Islam faith founded by the Prophet Muhammad. Therefore, Abraham is sometimes called the Father of Multitudes in Hebrew or the Father of Many Nations.

He is commanded by God to go and do a new thing, and Abraham obeys.

> *The LORD had said to Abram, "Go from your country, your people and your father's household to the land I will show you. I will make you into a great nation, and I will bless you: I will make your name great, and you will be a blessing. I will bless those who bless you, and whoever curses you I will curse; and all peoples on earth will be blessed through you."* Genesis 12:1-2

God also promised Abraham many sons. But dear Abe is having trouble believing Him. Many years have passed since the promise, and Sarah's pregnancy test doesn't show a pink plus sign. Abraham fears he will have to follow the custom of the day and leave his entire estate to his eldest servant, Eliezer.

God had other plans. He usually does.

> *Then the word of the LORD came to him: "This man will not be your heir, but a son who is your own flesh and blood will be your heir." He took him outside and said, "Look up at the sky and count the stars—if indeed you can count them." Then he said to him, "So shall your offspring be." Abram believed the LORD, and he credited it to him as righteousness.* Genesis 15: 4-6

However, there is a problem. Isn't there always?

Seriously. Let's take off the church mask and be real. Life isn't easy, especially in these confusing and fragile circumstances. Sarah (Sarai before the name change), Abraham's wife, still can't get pregnant.

In that day and time, being infertile was much more than agony or grief. It was detrimental. Sarah is desperate. Being childless meant a woman was scorned and shamed by her peers. She was mocked and in danger. Bearing a son isn't a want; it's a need. If her husband died and she had no son to take care of her, she would be destitute. With no source of income, indigent women had to resort to selling their bodies or going back home to family. Therefore, when a man died, his brother often stepped in and married his deceased brother's wife. She had no source of income without a husband or a son. Women were property. For the most part, they were a means of meeting a man's sexual needs and giving him heirs.

Sarah did what many of us do when God isn't giving us what we want. In her fear, torment, and yearning for a child, she took matters into her own hands. We might call her a control freak.

> *Now Sarai, Abram's wife, had borne him no children. But she had an Egyptian slave named Hagar; so, she said to Abram, "The Lord has kept me from having children. Go, sleep with my slave; perhaps I can build a family through her." Abram agreed to what Sarai said. So, after Abram had been living in Canaan ten years, Sarai his wife took her Egyptian slave Hagar and gave her to her husband to be his wife. He slept with Hagar, and she conceived.* Genesis 16:1-4

Now lift your chin off the floor and understand it was commonplace for women of that day who could not have children to hand over their servant to their husband as a substitute. A child conceived from that relationship was viewed as the wife's child, not the servant's.

In a state of desperation, after many years of waiting on God's promise, Sarah does what any despondent woman in her position at that time would do. She convinced herself it wasn't such a bad idea since God wasn't moving fast enough. She likely considered how busy God was dealing with all those wars going on, and He didn't have time for little ole Sarah (that's what I'd think). God isn't great at looking at the human calendar. She knows her ovaries are shrinking and her biological clock is ticking. Her hair is grey, and even the olive oil isn't working on her wrinkles anymore. God obviously needs help.

And when we allow swirling and anxious emotions to dominate the mind, it extinguishes faith.

Even though God had given Abraham a vision and proclamation that he would become a daddy, Sarah tells her husband to make a baby with her slave. And he complies.

Big Mistake, Abe. Big.

This is how Abraham's stepfamily began with disobedience to God.

I'm going to pause for a moment to share an extremely important statement regarding the theological "elephant in the room." Hear me clearly.

Not all stepfamilies are born out of sin and disobedience to God. This is an unjust, untrue, atrocious, and destructive categorization of shame. The church often brands this horrible stamp onto the foreheads of every stepfamily. It is wrong. It is sin. Each stepfamily has a different "ground zero" construction and establishment. Pharisees are the ones who proudly and arrogantly trademark a person as unclean. Christians should not.

Are some stepfamilies the result of sin? Yes. However, to label all people who are in a remarriage as living in opposition to God is untrue. This type of shame always starts in the same place - evil. It is the devil's desire to place a burden of shame on the family.

If your stepfamily is a result of sinful choices, go to God immediately. You cannot heal, form, or structure a healthy family that is built on sin and unholiness. But God...He can. He can restore your home and show you how to regain your dignity and life.

If you've been divorced or married a divorced person, you may have a distorted view about how God views you. As a remarried Christian, I understand. It took time, studying the Bible and learning from excellent teachers, for me to heal from the deception and unwarranted shame embedded in my brain.

My prayer is that this resource will do the same for you.

I know with first-hand experience that God is willing to draw near to any man or woman who sincerely cries out to Him. One night in 1980, I was abandoned, depressed, and suffering. When someone told me that Jesus loved me, I wanted to believe it was true but was afraid. I was raised in a strict church, so I knew just enough about God to understand He wants honesty. I prayed this prayer:

> *Jesus, I really don't know much about You. I know about church and church rules, but this concept of knowing you personally confuses me. If this is true, I desire to understand. I'm willing to hear that You are what I'm seeking, and I'm willing to learn. Please teach me. Please accept me; forgive me for my past, having lived without You. I want You in my heart and life. Today, I'm stepping forward and trusting. I believe that You, Jesus Christ, are the only Savior of the world. I want to live a life that honors You, God. And I'm humbling myself to say I don't know all the answers. Teach me the truth so my heart and mind will obey you. I surrender. Thank You for wanting me, forgiving me, and accepting me, Jesus. Amen.*

And He did accept me.

He will accept you too, even if your divorce was the result of your own sin. God forgives if you repent. Jesus shed his blood for all sin. Not just the ones the Church desires to be worthy. When we say that divorce cannot be forgiven, we are saying that divorce is more powerful than the blood of Jesus Christ. Are there long-term consequences to our sin? Definitely. That's why God hates it. However, He will not recoil from any person who sincerely seeks forgiveness.

Precious friend, if you have prayed this prayer as I did, know that all the angels in heaven are dancing. You are now a part of God's family, and the Holy Spirit, a part of His Trinity, resides within you. As you grow in Christ, He will teach you how to ask forgiveness for things and choices you made in opposition to His wisdom. This confession is a cleansing by the Holy Spirit of your mind, body, and soul. It is powerful! Liberating! Supernatural!

As you read, I encourage you to pray for God to give you the mind of Christ. This is vitally important because many of the teachings we will study are in direct opposition to the instruction of today's society. It will seem confusing. Social media, YouTube, television, and the Internet scream: "You are strong. Do what makes you happy. Don't worry about anyone else. You are what matters. Create your own truth. Let the Universe guide you. Karma is truth."

In comparison, Jesus tells us,

Relax. Rest in me. I'll teach you how to overcome. When you attempt to function in your own strength, you'll be overwhelmed and exhausted. I'm eager and willing to give you My strength in exchange for your weakness. Don't trust your emotions and feelings; they often lead you down the wrong path. Trust Me, Child. I want you to have peace. I'll never lead you toward destruction. (Author's paraphrase of Matthew 11:28-30.)

Jesus said, *"I am the way, and the truth, and the life. No one comes to the Father except through me."* John 14:6

Let's get back to Abe. For him, the situation with his women turns ugly very quickly.

When she knew she was pregnant, she began to despise her mistress. Then Sarai said to Abram, "You are responsible for the wrong I am suffering. I put my slave in your arms, and now that she knows she is pregnant, she despises me. May the LORD judge between you and me."

"Your slave is in your hands," Abram said. "Do with her whatever you think best." Then Sarai mistreated Hagar; so, she fled from her. Genesis 16:4-6

Hagar begins to taunt, sneer, and ridicule Sarah for being infertile. She's mocking her. She finally has something her owner longs for but can't have. This infuriates Sarah and unleashes a jealous rage, resentment, and hatred towards Haggar. And Hagar's swelling belly triggers an all-out vicious attack against Hagar, and—wait for it—her husband, Abraham.

Her frenzy of fury and envy morphs into an attack on her husband. The enraged Sarah does what many of us do. She blames Abraham. It's his fault that this baby, now growing so big and beautiful, is mocking her. And she expects him to do something about it—right now!

In desperation, Abraham finally throws up his hands and tells her to do what she wants with Hagar.

And Sarah wants Hagar—Out!

So, Sarah's abuse and tantrums finally drive Hagar to run away. At significant risk to herself, she leaves. It's safer than staying with this crazed infertile woman.

But God...

I love those two words. Don't you?

God steps in and shines when everything seems its darkest. He shows up when I shout out. And we read here that He does it for the weak, weary, and brokenhearted.

When we are desperate and have no shelter from the storm, He is our covering. He is our provider. And even though Hagar played a part in this nasty scenario with her sarcasm, God speaks to her.

It's crucial to remember she is not a Jew; she's an Egyptian. She isn't one of God's chosen people. This fact doesn't mean much to us in Western culture. We are taught that everyone is equal. In that culture, it means everything. She's an outsider. She's not worthy, except to God. He enters the situation with arms open wide and all His glory.

We see who He truly is while reaching out to this poor outcast and her son. In Hagar's wilderness journey, we witness one of God's most soothing, comforting, and promising attributes. He tells her He is "El Roi," "I'm the God who sees you."

> *The angel of the* LORD *found Hagar near a spring in the desert; it was the spring that is beside the road to Shur. And he said, "Hagar, slave of Sarai, where have you come from, and where are you going?"*
>
> *"I'm running away from my mistress Sarai," she answered. Then the angel of the Lord told her, "Go back to your mistress and submit to her." The angel added, "I will increase your descendants so much that they will be too numerous to count. "The angel of the* LORD *also said to her:*
>
> *"You are now pregnant, and you will give birth to a son. You shall name him Ishmael, for the* LORD *has heard of your misery. He will be a wild donkey of a man; his hand will be against everyone and everyone's hand against him, and he will live in hostility toward all his brothers. She gave this name to the Lord who spoke to her: "You are the God who sees me," for she said, "I have now seen the One who sees me." That is why the well was called Beer Lahai Roi; it is still there, between Kadesh and Bered. So, Hagar bore Abram a son, and Abram gave the name Ishmael to the son she had borne. Abram was eighty-six years old when Hagar bore him Ishmael.* Genesis 16:7-16

Over the years of working with hurting people, I have discovered that most have a deep desire to be heard and seen. That's all. They don't need solutions or instructions; they merely need to know that someone recognizes the pain.

When God sends His angel to Hagar, it demonstrates how His eyes and heart are upon her. She is seen. Perhaps for the first time in her life of slavery, someone is rescuing her rather than exploiting her. Her pain is palpable to God. And this sanctified and divine touch from her Creator via an angel is virtuous enough to turn her around. She follows His instructions. She goes back to the painful place occupied by Sarah and Abraham.

Once you have experienced a moment like this from God, it's not forgotten. Especially if they tend to be fearful or a worrier, as I am. I was never the same. It's only happened to me a few times (minus the angel), and it's difficult to describe. I sensed Him calling my name in such a profound yet intimate whisper. "I see you, Laura. You are not alone." It was as if the Holy Spirit wrapped Himself around me in a warm and cozy embrace. And a peace that I've never dreamed existed placed me in safety and stillness.

God wants to teach us how to trust Him. He often does that amid disaster, such as the one Hagar is experiencing.

Hagar goes back and has the baby; He is named Ishmael.

As time passes and Ishmael grows, God circles back to Abraham and reveals how He will fulfill His promise to Abraham. He will give him children through Sarah. He does this in His perfect timing and manner.

> *God also said to Abraham, "As for Sarai your wife, you are no longer to call her Sarai; her name will be Sarah. I will bless her and will surely give you a son by her. I will bless her so that she will be the mother of nations; kings of peoples will come from her."*

Abraham fell facedown; he laughed and said to himself, "Will a son be born to a man a hundred years old? Will Sarah bear a child at the age of ninety? Genesis 17:15-17

He's laughing at God. Good old Abe. He still hasn't learned his lesson, has he?

To be fair, he is 100. Sarah is 90. How can they have a baby? It's impossible, right?

Not by God's calculations.

Is anything too hard for the LORD? I will return to you at the appointed time next year, and Sarah will have a son." Genesis 18:14

And the beloved Isaac is born. Through his lineage, Jesus Christ, the Savior of the World, will arrive.

But back on the home front, the stepfamily tension increases.

The child grew and was weaned, and on the day Isaac was weaned Abraham held a great feast. But Sarah saw that the son whom Hagar the Egyptian had borne to Abraham was mocking, and she said to Abraham, "Get rid of that slave woman and her son, for that woman's son will never share in the inheritance with my son Isaac."

The matter distressed Abraham greatly because it concerned his son. But God said to him, "Do not be so distressed about the boy and your slave woman. Listen to whatever Sarah tells you, because it is through Isaac that your offspring will be reckoned. I will make the son of the slave into a nation also, because he is your offspring."

Older brother, Ishmael, is ridiculing his half-brother. Sarah's long-awaited precious son. And now she's infuriated—again. However, she has a child in her arms this time, and the momma bear emerges. She's in defense mode and doesn't need Hagar in her face every day as she once did.

She wants her gone. She's had enough.

Abe was in a conflicting mess, wasn't he? He's got two women who hate each other, and they each have his child. He's caught in the middle, and no matter what he does, someone is going to be angry with him.

And his kids will suffer. He knows it. It deeply burdens him with grief and misery.

He loves both sons. But the two baby mammas detest each other.

The sons are caught in the middle of the stepfamily warzone. A battle that has carried on in the Middle East to this day.

There is something comforting in knowing that a pillar of the Christian faith, in the genealogy of Jesus himself, knew what it was to encounter stepfamily stress. Abraham gets it. And his two wives who detest and loathe each other, do also.

With this type of animosity in the stepfamily, nobody wins.

We are thousands of years later, and these situations are as true today as they were for Abraham's family.

I can hear the husbands reading this book saying, "Abraham, the poor guy only did what his wife asked him to do. And then she blamed him. She rages at him for doing the very thing she demanded. A guy can't get a break."

And then under his breath, he whispers, "It's the same at my house."

Anyone who has experienced stepfamily tension, be it a husband, wife, grandparent child, parent, or in-laws, understands the high level of emotions. Right now, someone reading this is cheering, "Preach it, Sister. Preach it."

You're welcome.

Do you feel better? You should.

I do deeply sympathize with Sarah and Hagar. At the time, Sarah didn't realize her unwise decisions would cause extreme chaos for her future.

But hadn't God promised her that He would provide a son?

And, to some degree, poor Abraham does appear caught in the middle. However, he could have said no. He should have responded, "Honey, I know you want a baby. I'm sorry it's not happening. God said He will provide, and we are going to trust Him. I understand your fears and grief, and I'm here for you. I love you whether you have a baby or not. We are not going to step outside of God's direction. We will wait."

But (at least in the scenes we read) he didn't. And it created a long-lasting battle.

The War Between the Wives

It's time to bring this precious stepfamily into our present time. The clothes, food, languages, perfumes, and traditions are different. But the emotions are the same.

At least several times a month, I hear from a stepcouple who says something like this:

"My husband's ex-wife is high conflict, vindictive, and crazy. She does everything she can to make our lives as miserable as possible intentionally", stepmom states.

"I think she's bi-polar," husband adds.

Stepmoms, I understand. For thirty years, my husband's former spouse, whom I call an ex-wife-in-law, was a constant in my life and my face. She is now deceased. There is no minimizing the aggression and resentment I encountered from my husband's former spouse during my stepmom journey. In the first few years, there were many times I wanted to run away or wished she would move.

Critical thoughts regarding her choices, parenting style, accusations, decisions, and spending habits would roll around in my brain until I thought I'd explode. She frequently made my life much more complicated, inconvenient, and taxing than I could have imagined. I tried to respond to her in a godly manner, but I often failed. My heart wanted to build a bridge, and I desired to respect her as the mom of my two stepsons. Then she would do something hurtful, and my emotions began to rule my actions. I'd responded negatively. I hadn't learned how to take those thoughts captive and make them obey God's path. In hindsight, I probably could have done more to reconcile our differences.

Although not as frequent as females, dads and stepdads can also have a disdain for each other. Controlling the emotions that come with the stepfamily dynamic requires immense prayer, discipline, and desire.

Here's a statement I hear from stepdads.

> *"My wife's former husband does nothing to take care of his children properly,"* the stepdad explained. *"I pay for all their extra-curricular activities at school, I buy them clothes, and I'm the one that takes them to football practice. He's a horrible father. And yet he still becomes furious if one of his kids accidentally calls me dad."*

This stepdad is upset because, in his opinion, the biological dad isn't stepping up. He could be right. However, he could be reacting negatively because he's overly sensitive. The dad might perceive his child support payments as proof that he's a good father. Each situation is different and unique. Men can become resentful, jealous, and angry about stepfamily situations, too. Women and stepmoms are not the only ones who have hostility toward the other home.

In my own circumstance, it took several years of turmoil before I embraced the truth that I couldn't control my husband's former spouse or her actions. I had to find a way to stop allowing her comments, attitude, and even occasional lies to dictate the condition of my heart and the atmosphere in my home. I had to cease responding like a puppet on a string when her choice frustrated me.

It took time and a willing, teachable heart, but eventually, I was able to incarcerate my enraged thoughts.

Stepfamilies God's Way

I finally cried out to God and sincerely asked Him how to victoriously live the stepfamily life—His way. He's so patient. I don't understand why or how He is, but it's true.

God graciously began to teach me these insights:

Willing to Become Willing

A stepparent must be eager to obtain a mind at peace. The desire for a ceasefire is the first step toward victory. This may sound trite or obvious; however, there is a vast difference between desiring something and being willing to do the work to make it happen. Praying, *Lord, I don't want to do this, but "I'm willing to become willing"* is a great place to start.

Get Quiet with God

Learning how to stop the chaos in our brains takes time and intentionality. It's imperative to spend time alone with

God and speak the truth (out loud if necessary) regarding the emotions and feelings the stepfamily life has stirred. If a person has a mind prone to self-shame and self-hatred, it can trigger jealousy, feeling abandoned, or worthless.

While deep inside most stepparents desire to love their stepkids, it doesn't prevent the thoughts or emotions from becoming unloving or unkind. Ask God to reveal if this is occurring.

Why? It's the key to healing. He will not and cannot mend a wound you don't—or won't—admit exists. It's like mold sprouting in a basement. In darkness, it reproduces and prospers. But when God's sunlight shines into dark crevices, the decay is destroyed so restoration and recovery can begin.

God knows what created the damage to our self-worth, hearts, and minds. He even grasps the hidden wounds not yet discovered.

Healing the intimate pain is God's job. Not mine. My job is to be willing to give Him my heart and mind, including all the trauma. He won't pluck it out. He's a gentle God. He waits for us to be ready. I'm required to hand it over.

This requires placing myself in specific biblical classes, prayers, and teachings on how God heals a wounded person. We rarely do it alone. He typically brings others who have already healed around us.

When I discovered that much of the stepfamily hurt I was experiencing was rooted in my own innermost fears and insecurities, everything changed. Now I knew the why. Knowing the why led me to learning the how to overcome.

Discover What's Normal

We just read about Sarah becoming an infuriated, exasperated, raging wife. Why? What drove her to those over-the-top emotions?

The answer to that question is the same today. When a spouse has a child with another person, it hurts. When the remarriage already comes with kids, the mind accepts this as truth. We didn't anticipate how that fact would create bitterness and anger. It's normal to be jealous of our precious mate having a former love intimate enough to create a baby. They have shared an experience that the new couple has not. These emotions are typical. But we can't stay there.

My issue was rooted in fear. I needed to be in control. This need can be traced to my own childhood and my parents' divorce. The fear of having no control in a situation caused anxiety and anger to stir within me. My childhood experiences taught me that when I wasn't in control, bad things could happen. As an adult walking with God, I needed to learn there are many things, including an ex-wife, I couldn't control. This is life. God is in control; I am not.

Accept what you can't change. You don't have to like it, but you do have to accept it. Your spouse has kids with another person. Period.

Be Honest

God can handle our anger. We don't need to be afraid to tell Him how we really feel.

Let it out.

"Lord, I hate all of this. And to be honest, I feel a bit deceived. Although I love my husband, I didn't know being a stepparent would be this hard. There are some days I'm so frustrated, hurt, and rejected I don't care if my marriage survives.

Or

I'm scared. I have already lived through one divorce; I don't want another. I don't recognize myself anymore. I've become someone who is mean and nasty, and I don't even know how it happened.

Or

I don't like my life. This is not what I thought the future would look like. If I had known on my wedding day that this would be my life, I wouldn't have done it.

Sometimes, we need a friend to hear us say these things. Another stepparent who understands the dynamic is often a great choice. Find or start a stepmom or stepfamily group to help. When you hear others say the same thing you are thinking and feeling, it brings relief. You understand this is a normal stepfamily reaction.

God hears and sees, just like He did with Hagar. He wants your honesty.

Lose Your Mind

Typically, thought patterns need to be changed. It can be thoughts about myself, kids, a spouse, stepkids, the ex-spouse, the spouse's ex-spouse, extended family, and in-laws. If not, the same vicious cycle continues.

How does that occur? Through numerous studies and exploring various resources, I have learned how and why God desires to transform my mind. He didn't want critical thoughts taking over my brain and bringing turmoil into my life any more than I did.

> *Do not be conformed to this world, but be transformed by the renewal of your mind, that by testing you may discern what is the will of God, what is good and acceptable and perfect.* Romans 12:2 (ESV)

God's method for mind renewal is perfect and practical. It requires patience because it's a process. There is no abracadabra with a magic wand. It is not a one-and-done for the rest of your life. New circumstances and life encounters (stepfamily or not) will arise, creating a need to backtrack and review again. Thinking like Christ, taking thoughts hostage, and responding like Jesus did is only possible by the power of the Holy Spirit. The more the mind is renewed to react and think like Jesus, the more natural, instinctive, and spontaneous it becomes.

Don't misunderstand. It's always a battle. The mind will instinctively gravitate toward self-seeking responses and actions. But God teaches how to overcome that egotistical and human response.

Set Margins

It's not uncommon to possess a distorted definition of Christ's characteristics. In our culture, we have perverted the words mercy, love, and grace (all godly attributes) to mean ignore, tolerate, and endorse a person's destructive choices.

In certain circumstances, it's not unloving or unkind to say no. God does it all the time. The key question to ask yourself is, "What's my motive?" If I'm refusing because I want to punish, retaliate, or make someone suffer, it's not a godly action. When an ex-spouse is involved, the fury, jealousy, and angst can make it difficult to discern a true motive. We can deceive ourselves into believing we're doing it for the kids. When in reality, it's driven by a desire for revenge.

Setting healthy, holy boundaries in a stepfamily is a good thing. The struggle occurs when discerning the motive. Ask yourself: Am I saying no to punish the person? Or am I saying no because I've gotten hurt by this person before, and it's fine for me to protect my heart, mind, and emotions.

Eyes Wide Open

Here's a final and the most sacrificial of the steps listed.

Ask God to allow you to see the situation through the eyes of the person who is hurting you.

An example could be: Lord, help me to see this situation through my stepchild's mother's eyes. Give me her perspective. Even though I'm angry with her, and she has hurt me before, I don't trust her, but I still desire to see this through her lens. Give me compassion for her. I don't know why she does the hurtful things she does, but you do. I don't know the wounds she may have, but you do. Give me Your sight right now. Stop me from seeing this situation through my own dimmed lens. Instead, open the eyes of my heart. I need to see what You see."

To illustrate this step, let's go back to Abraham's stepfamily. Notice how the two women make remarkably similar choices? Both Sarah and Hagar are stubborn and prideful. They refuse to humble themselves and admit, "I'm in this catastrophe because I threw gasoline on the fire. Me. I did it—no one else. This might not have occurred if I had kept my big mouth shut. I let my emotions get the best of me."

Neither is willing to admit they have played a role in the problem. It's more important to be right than at peace. It's essential to be smug and superior toward my adversary. My goal is to be proven right and justified. I don't care if it creates more problems. I deserve justice.

In my years of working with stepfamilies, I have seen many similarities between today's blended family and Abraham's. Each family member is desperate to be heard and validated.

And yet to live like Jesus means extending consideration, sensitivity, and courtesy to another. When a person's main objective is being right, they shouldn't be mystified when the battle rages.

Not every adult in the stepfamily has equal fault when there is conflict. And responding like Jesus doesn't guarantee a gloriously happy family ending like the Brady Bunch.

Jesus said no sometimes. When God told him to turn and walk away from certain people, He did. The goal isn't to become a wimpy doormat for people to take advantage of us. But instead, we have discovered a better way to respond when the battle rages. Rather than allowing our emotions, insecurities, anger, and fears to dictate our responses, we will pause long enough to consider a more productive response.

If we learn nothing else from this Old Testament stepfamily, it should be what can occur when we step outside of God's umbrella of wisdom, purpose, and direction. The temptation to take matters into our own hands can be disastrous.

Running ahead of God, rather than waiting on Him, typically results in painful consequences.

God is wiser than we are. It's as simple as that. In the same way, you would never intentionally harm or withhold anything good from your own child; God never intentionally withholds good from us.

Faith is not a feeling. It's a choice.

And for those who have surrendered their life to Christ—it's a promise.

> *For the Lord God is a sun and shield; the Lord bestows favor and honor; no good thing does he withhold from those whose walk is blameless."* Psalm 84:11

Did you know the same grace and forgiveness God extended to Abraham's family and stepfamily is available to you and your stepfamily? It's true.

God loves your stepfamily.

And He died to prove it. He died to heal it. He died to resurrect it.

WHAT DO WE LEARN FROM THIS STEPFAMILY?

Much can be learned from this stepfamily. Each adult in the family made poor, fear-driven, self-centered choices that led to pain for everyone, including the kids. We live in a society where it's no one's business what I choose to do. We reject and discard with anger the truth that our choices affect others.

Here is a summary of what we can learn from Abraham and his family.

Abraham's Unwise Choices:

- He didn't trust God with the future.
- He didn't say no to his wife when she grew tired of waiting for God and decided to speed up the baby-making process.
- He refused to be the spiritual leader in his own home and allowed Sarah's rage to direct his actions.
- He neglected to man up and resolve the hostility between Sarah and Hagar, the mother of his child.
- He abandoned Hagar and his child by failing to rescue them from Sarah's wrath.
- He continues with a complacent "peace at all costs" mentality, placing Hagar and his own son in danger.

Sarah's Unwise Choices:

- She didn't trust God with the future.
- She allowed the fear of infertility to dictate her actions.
- She refused to take responsibility for her decisions and wouldn't own the role she played in creating the predicament.
- She permitted the shame of barrenness to embed hatred and jealousy for her husband's child and Hagar.
- She returns evil for evil towards the mean girl when her adversary, Hagar, becomes a mocking bully.
- She disrespected her husband by banishing his child and the child's mother.

Hagar's Unwise Choices:

- Although she should be given extra grace because she's a slave and not one of God's chosen people, she still needs to be accountable for her poor choices.
- After becoming pregnant, she intentionally and gleefully humiliates Sarah.
- She belittles her mistress. She bites the hand that is feeding and providing for her unborn child.
- She disrespected her baby's father by insulting his wife.
- She jeopardized her child's entire future for the momentary pleasure of ridiculing Sarah.
- She refused to take responsibility for her decisions and wouldn't own the role she played in creating the predicament.
- She ran from her problems rather than resolving them.

HOW DOES LEARNING ABOUT *THIS* STEPFAMILY STRENGTHEN *MY* STEPFAMILY?

1. Which character in this stepfamily is most relatable for you? How does this make you feel?
2. What do Abraham and Sarah teach us about overcoming stepfamily frustration and resentment?
3. Looking at each family member, how could they have done things more productively? What outcome might have been the result?
4. Can you name a time when you made a poor stepfamily choice?
5. After reading the Stepfamilies God's Way section in this chapter, what steps can you take to prevent that from happening again?
6. We are told Hagar is not an Israelite (a believer in God), but rather an Egyptian, someone outside the faith. Should she be held to the same standard as Abraham and Sarah? What about the non-Christians in your family, the other home, and previous family circle? Should they be given a different type of grace or response?
7. Does God hold Christians to a different standard than a non-believer? What if the person is my spouse, ex-spouse, ex-spouse's new family, stepkids, or in-laws? What can I do or pray that will help that person know Christ?
8. Who do you believe suffered the most because of the poor choices of Abraham, Sarah, and Hagar? Why?
9. Who/what is the most affected in my blended family when I choose to let emotions, rather than God, dictate my thoughts, behavior, and words?

10. After looking at Abraham's family, what things am I doing that are similar? What specific steps can I take to help change or ease the struggles we face in our stepfamily?

Do I have unresolved issues and/or pain from my past? Am I allowing them to affect my marriage and my stepfamily? Who can I trust to help me discover the correct answer if I'm unsure?

PRAYER

Lord, I never thought about you loving my stepfamily. Things are so complex that I assumed you gave up on us. Forgive me. I now realize I have a distorted view of who you are and how you love. Thank you, Lord, for seeing me in the wilderness. Thank you for loving me even when I'm not loveable or beautiful on the inside or outside. Help me to stop wanting others to change. Teach me to focus on the only one that I control —me. When jealousy, resentment, and anger threaten to destroy my family and my peace, help me to take that thought captive.

If I'm being honest, I hate that my spouse has a previous life and partner. I want him/her to disappear. I want to pretend they don't exist. Lord, I pray for my spouse's former partner. I ask you to cover him/her with your love and mercy. If he/she doesn't know you as the savior of the world, I pray that today, you would put someone in his/her path to share the truth. I pray you would give him/her a heart to hear the truth, and they would know how deeply you love them.

Teach me, Lord, how to treat this person with godly respect, even when I do not get it in return. Let the healing begin with me. Help me not to wait for the other person to do the right thing. Show me how to take one baby step forward to responding as you would to him/her. I know that in each circumstance, this will look different. That's not my job. That's your job. My job is to lay down my sword, my anger, my bitterness, my revenge, my pettiness, and the desire to retaliate.

I need you, Lord. This week, I will take intentional steps toward allowing you to make me like Christ. Whenever my mind thinks of the situations, person or persons in my stepfamily who upset me, I will pray for them, rather than allow my thoughts to brew into exasperation.

I believe in you. I trust you. I surrender to your way and not my own. Amen.

~ 2 ~

OVERCOMING REJECTION

Laban, Jacob, Rebekah, and Leah

Just like many of us who enter stepfamily living, Jacob had no idea what he was getting into. Initially, he did not even know he would end up with a stepfamily. But the Bible is filled with family members, step or not, who are manipulative and deceptive.

We must consistently remember that in Biblical times, the sole purpose of a wife was to produce heirs—particularly sons. A woman's value, worth, and significance was singularly attached to her ability to produce sons. When a wife was infertile, the shame, disgrace, and humiliation were overwhelming. It also caused dishonor and discredit to her husband and his family.

Isaac is Abraham and Sarah's first son together. He married Rebekah, and we now enter the world of their son Jacob, Abraham's grandson.

Jacob is seeking a wife. And Isaac wants to make sure she's a godly girl.

> *"You must not take a wife from the Canaanite women. Arise, go to Paddan-aram to the house of Bethuel your*

mother's father, and take as your wife from there one of the daughters of Laban your mother's brother." Genesis 28:1-2

Dad understands the significance of wisely choosing a wife. His son's spouse will have a massive impact on his future.

The same is true today.

Therefore, Isaac sends Jacob a long distance away to his mother's family, where he can find a proper godly wife. He doesn't want his son mixing, marrying, and having babies with the ungodly women in the neighborhood. To our culture, this sounds racist, judgmental, snobby, and unloving. It's not. It's God's command. And God never commands without a cause. His formidable reasons sometimes appear confusing, but His plans are always perfect.

The same God gives Christians today a similar command. His spousal boundary is not based on color, money, status, or culture. Rather, God wants His people to evaluate the potential spouse's heart and mind. He tells His followers, "Don't make a vow (marriage, commitment) to a person who doesn't have the same understanding, salvation, and surrender to Jesus as you do."

> *"Don't team up with those who are unbelievers. How can righteousness be a partner with wickedness? How can light live with darkness? What harmony can there be between Christ and the devil? How can a believer be a partner with an unbeliever? And what union can there be between God's temple and idols?"* 2 Corinthians 6:14-16 (NLT)

God is trying to protect His people from pain. If one spouse worships Christ and the other does not, it can destroy the unity in the home. The moral compass of the family will be divided. Marriage is hard enough without adding the tension of being pulled in two different directions on vital decisions. A person who doesn't follow Christ uses society or feelings to decide what is right and wrong. The one who looks to God's words, the Bible, as their parameters has vastly different approaches and perspectives on life.

When it came to wife picking, Isaac knew and believed God's instructions. He obeyed God. He wanted his son to do the same. So, he sent Jacob away to his brother-in-law Laban's property to find a wife. And Jacob fell in love.

> *"Now Laban had two daughters. The name of the older was Leah, and the name of the younger was Rachel. Leah's eyes were weak, but Rachel was beautiful in form and appearance. Jacob loved Rachel. And he said, "I will serve you seven years for your younger daughter Rachel." Laban said, "It is better that I give her to you than that I should give her to any other man; stay with me." So, Jacob served seven years for Rachel, and they seemed to him but a few days because of the love he had for her."* Genesis 29:16-20 (ESV)

However, Uncle Laban is a ruthless, deceitful man. He pulls several dirty tricks on Jacob. The biggest starts on the wedding night. He switches his daughters.

> *"So Laban gathered together all the people of the place and made a feast. But in the evening, he took his daughter Leah and brought her to Jacob, and he went into her. Laban gave his female servant Zilpah to his daughter Leah to be her servant. And in the morning, behold, it was Leah! And Jacob said to Laban, "What is this you have done to me? Did I not serve with you for Rachel? Why then have you deceived me?"* Genesis 29: 22-25 (HCSB)

After seven years of working for him, Uncle Laban throws a big wedding for Jacob and his bride. However, the next morning after waking, Jacob discovers that lying next to him is—Leah—not Rachel. He is married to Leah, the homely older sister, not Rachel, his gorgeous true love.

He is stunned, outraged, and devastated. Who wouldn't be?

How Is That Even Possible?

It's extremely difficult in our sex obsessed society to understand how this astonishing undertaking of "switching brides" could occur. To understand Jacob's plight, we must become familiar with the bridal ensemble in Jacob's day.

In Biblical times, the bride was covered head-to-toe with heavy veils. It's likely even her hands and arms were covered. At night, it would be very dark in the honeymoon tent. As a virgin, she would be shy and frightened to experience her first sexual encounter. It was not uncommon for a groom to see his new bride for the first time in morning's light.

Contrast to today. If you have ever watched the television show Say Yes to the Dress, you know that modern bridal attire often leaves little to the imagination. Not only is the bride's face showing, but most of her other parts too.

Laban knew how his daughter would be covered on her wedding day, and that made for an easy switch-a-roo. Laban sought what he wanted. And his desire was for his older daughter to be married first, so he deceived Jacob. And as badly as I feel for Jacob, my soft heartstrings pull for Leah, the unwanted sister.

Can you imagine the overwhelming sorrow in this woman's heart when she knows she isn't the one her husband loves, desires, and craves? She's so unlovable and undesirable that her own father must deceive the groom to get her a husband.

Unloved. Unwanted. Humiliated. Shamed.

Remember those words, as they play a vital role in the future of this family.

Fast forward to years later, Laban finally gives Rachel to Jacob to marry.

We read that she is his true love.

"Jacob went into Rachel also, and he loved Rachel more than Leah, and served Laban for another seven years."
Genesis 29:30 (ESV)

As babies begin to arrive, the bitter resentment between the two sisters turns into a catfight. That's when the fur really starts to fly. Leah, the scorned one, can have children. Rachel, the beloved one, cannot.

Big problem.

Even though thousands of years have passed since these two sisters lived, some things don't change. In my thirty years of ministry, I've observed that a woman's greatest struggles still center around the fear associated with abandonment, dismissal, irrelevance, and worthlessness.

The unison cry I receive from stepmoms is, "I feel like an outsider, even in my own home. I'm lonely. I don't matter. My thoughts, feelings, and opinions are discarded. My husband focuses on doing whatever his kids want and keeping the peace at all costs with his ex-spouse happy. My feelings are completely disregarded. I am a nobody to my stepkids and sometimes my husband."

Profound, isn't it?

Can't you just hear Leah saying the same thing to Jacob? She longs to be loved by her husband.

Jealousy Flourishes

And here is where the sly seed of jealousy embeds itself deeply into her soul.

> *"When Rachel saw that she bore Jacob no children, she envied her sister. She said to Jacob, "Give me children, or I shall die!" Jacob's anger was kindled against Rachel, and he said, "Am I in the place of God, who has withheld from you the fruit of the womb?"* Genesis: 30:1-2 (ESV)

Jacob's response to his beloved, Rachael, discloses more than one might realize at first glance. His burning frustration with God is exposed. And his intolerance and dismissal of his wife's pain and grief divulges a nasty side of him when things don't go his way.

The jealousy between the women revealed in these passages could be xeroxed from a modern stepfamily handbook.

Jealousy, envy, resentment, and possessiveness rear their ugly heads proclaiming, "He's mine."

Today's emotions aren't always linked to barrenness or children as they were in the Old Testament. Other battlegrounds create a warzone and are fought upon today.

Anything that ignites the comparison between the former union and the current marriage can set off the fireworks. A trigger that chants, "You experienced that happy moment for the first time with your ex, and now it has damaged having it with me," can create hostile competition.

It might be a favorite vacation spot that hubby had with his former spouse, a sport the wife enjoyed with her former husband, or a mission trip the former couple experienced together. It could be a death, a job, a sexual experience, or an adventure. Former times with the previous partner, both good and bad, can create a competition where no one wins. It's not uncommon in a blended family to think of your spouse and consider, "You had that with him/her, and you don't have that with me, and I'm very upset about it."

People can find the slightest thing to resent when it comes to the previous partner or current spouse. Women can be the most loving thing God ever created. The opposite is also true. Put mom and stepmom in a boxing ring together, and blood could appear. It can get very ugly.

This isn't an attempt to dismiss, or trivialize, how reprehensible a former spouse (male or female) can be. After 20 years in stepfamily ministry, I have observed how men are better at coping with their wife's former partner, than women do dealing with an ex-wife.

Men can be naive when it comes to the deep-seated hatred an ex-spouse and a current wife can carry for one another. They know the claws are out because they feel the lacerations. But they rarely understand why. He just wants peace.

An unwise man will accuse his wife of behaving "like a child." Guess how well that goes over?

And that's basically what Jacob is doing here. Exasperated, he throws up his hands emotionally and yells at Rebekah, "What do you want me to do about it?"

We witness Rachel's response as crying, lamenting, and fuming over her circumstances. And then, what does she do? Wait for it. Who does she blame for her predicament? God? Her ovaries? The universe? No! She blames her husband.

It would be funny if it didn't hit so close to home. He's the one who wanted only her as his wife to begin with.

Jacob was a victim too. It wasn't just the two sisters. He was tricked into the whole chaotic mess by his own uncle. Yet, this does not excuse his reprehensible response to Rachel. And although he didn't love Leah, he obviously had no problem having sexual intimacy and children with her.

Stepfamilies, hear me. It's common. Sometimes, we blame our spouse for things that are not within his/her control. It's crucial to calm down, step back, and look at the root of the problem rather than allowing our emotions to dictate behavior.

As we continue to observe Leah, something in her drastically changes. She develops a new attitude. Her thoughts aren't nearly as much about her husband or getting him to love her. That disappointment appears to have hardened her heart, and winning her husband's affection isn't her goal anymore.

> *When Leah saw that she had ceased bearing children, she took her servant Zilpah and gave her to Jacob as a wife. Then Leah's servant Zilpah bore Jacob a son. And Leah said, "Good fortune has come!" so she called his name Gad. Leah's servant Zilpah bore Jacob a second son. And Leah said, "Happy am I! For women have called me happy."* Genesis 30:9-13 (ESV).

Two more sons. And even though she didn't physically birth them herself, she's extremely happy. Maybe too happy?

Hmmm... something is shifting. We see Leah's focus is recalculating. Revenge is the new passion. She draws her son into a new thickening plot to hurt her rival.

> *In the days of wheat harvest Reuben went and found mandrakes in the field and brought them to his mother*

Leah. Then Rachel said to Leah, "Please give me some of your son's mandrakes." But she said to her, "Is it a small matter that you have taken away my husband? Would you take away my son's mandrakes also?" Rachel said, "Then he may lie with you tonight in exchange for your son's mandrakes." Genesis 30:14-15 (ESV)

It's important to understand what mandrakes are and why they were special. *Mandrake (genus Mandragora) is a genus of six species of hallucinogenic plants in the nightshade family (Solanaceae) native to the Mediterranean region and the Himalayas. The plants are particularly noted for their potent roots, which somewhat resemble the human form and have a long history of use in religious and superstitious practices.* [3] People of that day believed the plants were beneficial to, and valuable for creating fertility in infertile women.

Some Bible translations use the word flowers, but this gives us the wrong impression of what is happening. This isn't about a bouquet of roses. These plants had a purpose; they were a bargaining chip.

You give me the plants that aid in impregnation, I'll give you the man.

You will be hard-pressed to find a better example of stepfamily competition and rivalry than right here. Leah, who has been slighted throughout her entire marriage, snaps at Rachel over some plants. Is it about foliage? NO! It's about insatiable greed. It's a means to an end.

When a person becomes focused on revenge, and a root of bitterness has harnessed the heart, we transform into

---

3   https://www.britannica.com/plant/mandrake-Mandragora-genus

slaves. The master? Hatred. It owns us. We no longer care who gets wounded in the crossfire.

This is how many blended families respond to one another. It becomes a competition.

"I am the adult the child favors. I'm the better parent. I WIN!"

It sounds immature, foolish, and sad when read, doesn't it?

And does the kid really care who wins? Did Reuben care whether his mother shared the plants? It's possible he witnessed his mother weeping and shunned. He may have compassion for her situation and wanted to help. Typically, the child doesn't care about the fight between his parents and stepparents unless or until it creates stress, or a loyalty bind, in his/her own life.

Leah's plot is revealed.

> *That evening when Jacob came in from the fields, Leah told him, "You're sleeping with me tonight. I hired you with my son's love flowers."* Genesis 30:16

POW! Her words are a humiliating punch in the face. And that's her goal. Leah goes for the jugular. Or should I say—his man parts.

She degrades, disrespects, and emasculates him with three simple words: "I hired you."

When a woman feels belittled, ridiculed, and rejected, things can get ugly—fast. Hence the quote, "There is no fury like a woman scorned."

Now it's time to become vulnerable—my own confession. In my younger years, I had a critical attitude about many things, particularly my husband. It took me a long time to overcome it. It is the personality trait I possess that

I hate the most. On occasion, I slip up and do it. But I've become much better at taming my tongue.

Reflecting On Our Past

My own childhood was filled with intense criticism. Men were habitually the target of venomous condemnation in my home. I thought this way because I observed it. I thought it natural and acceptable—sometimes even praiseworthy – to humiliate a man. As a young adult, I came to know Christ and discovered this tongue-lashing was unbecoming for a Christian woman. I wanted to stop and consistently asked the Holy Spirit to teach me to 'zip it before I lip it'. Over time, and with discipline, He taught me a different way to think and respond.

God is always willing to answer a sincere prayer to become more like Him. Sometimes, our pain is so severe we feel we can't move towards healing. Or we don't want to stop because it triggers pleasure. Years ago, I heard a speaker say, "Pain pursues pleasure." It's true. We do things because we get something out of it, or we wouldn't do it.

We see our sister Leah; she is anguished and rejected. These palpable emotions instilled a desire to retaliate. And because we know our spouse intimately, we go directly to his/her most vulnerable place. It's a dagger to the heart.

My spouse is supposed to be my "safe place" to fall. The one person I can trust, rely on, and run to when I'm devastated.

He/she is never to be a bully, a destroyer, a manipulator, or the crusher of my heart. However, if my spouse hasn't healed from the wounds inflicted on him/her, they can become the most unsafe person in my circle. Deep damage done to a spouse's heart can turn him/her into a severely immature, self-centered, and cruel person.

We must be real. If Christians are to be anything, it's truthful. We are all sinners. We will have a bad day, week, or season when we are drained or tested. It's normal to be ugly sometimes and say or do something to our spouse that isn't godly and loving. We fail.

What we are describing and illustrated by Leah isn't a bad day. Leah's heart had changed toward Jacob. She gave up on trying to get her husband to love her. She was done.

The Numb Spouse

And the emotional place where Leah now resides is a perfect example of what happens when a spouse repeatedly abuses, criticizes, disregards, neglects, or dominates a spouse. Each day, with each criticism, the spouse dies a little more inside. Eventually, the spouse is numb.

Ignoring, tolerating, or dismissing hurtful and insulting behavior from a spouse isn't love, respect, compassion, or kindness. When a man or woman repeatedly insults, criticizes, and demeans a spouse, and he/she never suffers a consequence for those sinful actions, the marriage is in serious trouble. The victim becomes a contributing factor to the wickedness occurring in the relationship by refusing to say "no more." True devotion, holy affection, and godly love don't pretend or dismiss a spouse's toxic or manipulative behavior. True love, the type that Christ displays, knows to hold the spouse accountable for sinful behavior. It's typically the only way the person repents, seeks accountability, and starts to truly live.

"My husband doesn't hit me with his fists, but with his words," stepmom Karla shared. "He flies into a rage when I attempt to discuss our stepfamily issues. I've learned to keep everything to myself to avoid his outburst of anger. I don't tell him how I feel or how I'm shrinking inside. I'm growing to hate my life and my stepkids. I guess I just married the wrong person."

If Karla's husband doesn't wake up and realize what is happening in his marriage, she will likely leave.

In stepfamilies, this also occurs when the biological children habitually disrespect and humiliate their mother or father. The stepparent can develop a disdain and disgust for their spouse.

"My wife lets her sons treat her like dirt. They call her names and walk all over her. If I step in and try to defend her, she sides with them. I hate watching them treat her this way, but I feel my hands are tied. I just go out to the garage and work on my car to take my mind off it.

This husband walks away, but a different emotion is often stirred for women. They are repulsed when a husband allows his children to disrespect him. And that abhorrence transfers into their intimacy and sex life.

"I just can't stand it. And I'm getting concerned over how it is causing the feelings for my husband to change," stepmom Kloee declared.

"The way my stepkids speak to my husband is appalling. He gives them anything they want, and it's never enough," she continued.

"They belittle and humiliate him, and it makes me nauseous. He never corrects them, and there are no consequences for their actions. Sometimes, he even rewards them. I know he fears losing them to their mom, but I'm losing all respect for him. It has started to affect our intimacy because I'm so turned off by his pathetic, spineless inability to parent his kids. I no longer want to have sex because he's acting like such an immature indulgent baby, and not a man."

If I had a dollar for every stepmom who has said this, I could live in Hawaii—on the beach, in a six-bedroom villa. Men don't usually carry these emotions into the bedroom, but women do.

When a parent permits their kids to misbehave and doesn't correct them, it negatively affects the blended family marriage. And the spouse loses respect.

This is a complicated and multifaceted subject requiring a deep dive. However, Leah's change in attitude toward her husband is an excellent illustration of how a spouse can go from being passionately in love to disdain over time. It is a warning to be heeded.

Many of us have a distorted view of marital love and need to learn how to set healthy, godly, loving boundaries so that our marital connection doesn't get lost. This is a journey—not a sprint.

Rachel eventually does have a child. His name is Joseph, and then his younger brother Benjamin comes along.

This stepfamily has much more to teach us, but for now, let's stop and consider what is happening with our Old Testament friends.

Ask God to transform your mind so you think like Jesus. It's not a "one and done." It's an ongoing process, a voyage. And it's mighty! Once you experience the transformation from man's puny perspective to God's outlook, you'll be eager to seek the mind of Christ again and again.

WHAT DO WE LEARN FROM THIS STEPFAMILY?

- Each family member adds to the problem, frustration, resentment, and anger. It's not one person who is causing all the issues.

- Spouses from ancient times battled many of the same things we do today.
- When personal pain (Laban's deception and Rebekah's infertility) is dismissed and left unhealed, it can teach us to react in unloving ways, making the situation worse.
- Intentional wounds from a spouse often fracture trust, intimacy, passion, and the bond within the relationship.
- Repeated abuse, neglect, lack of boundaries with the kids, and indifference may cause a spouse to become emotionally numb and physically (even sexually) distant in the relationship.
- What is your reaction to the discovery that Leah, a woman who lived centuries ago, had the same cry, emotions, fear, and sorrow as many wives do today?
- Does it bring comfort?
- What can we learn about God from this?
- How did Leah's focus change because Jacob didn't appreciate or desire her?
- Who is she trying to please instead? Why?
- Do I blame my spouse for situations he/she didn't choose?
- Why do I do this? What can I do to become more aware of unjustly punishing my spouse?
- What are specific ways I can become more aware of unjustly punishing my spouse?
- Speak to your spouse. Ask: Do I do things like Jacob does to Leah? Do you feel I bully, neglect, or dismiss you? And then LISTEN without defending yourself. REALLY allow your spouse to speak. And, Spouse, share your response in a calm, kind, non-accusatory manner.

HOW DOES LEARNING ABOUT *THIS* STEPFAMILY STRENGTHEN *MY* STEPFAMILY?

It's normal for the ex and current spouse (favored one) to have a contemptuous relationship. This is more present for women than for men. Women tend to be more jealous of an ex-wife or the new wife. They must choose whether to continue the fight or let it go. You can only control your part in the relationship.

- Competition is normal in stepfamilies, but it's also destructive. What drives such fierce competition in our home?
- Is my immediate response to blame the ex for most of the issues in our home? Does this autopilot response prevent me from considering there may be more to the situation?
- Who wins or loses when we allow competition between homes? What can I do to lessen the issues?
- Has there been a time when you said something to your spouse and knew it was a knife to the heart? What did you hope to accomplish with those words or actions? Did it have the outcome you desired?
- When is the last time I prayed for my spouse's former spouse?
- Do I accuse my spouse of not loving my kids? Do I unjustly judge his/her heart or intentions?
- If I struggle to discipline my kids, what can I do to learn a better way?
- Why do I struggle to let go of the anger and resentment over the fact that my spouse has children from a previous marriage?

Time for a Pause

After looking at two stepfamilies from the Bible, let's add a few more self-reflections

Look at our own stepfamily for a moment. Ask yourself:

- How am I responding to the things I have already learned? Why am I reading this book? What do I hope to learn?
- Am I becoming angry as I learn about stepfamily dynamics? Am I willing to let God help me with my stepfamily connections, even if I need to change?
- Is what we are doing in our blended family working to create a peaceful home?
- Is my spouse losing respect for me?
- Do we have goals on how to create and maintain a safe home where everyone feels heard and we are considerate of each other?
- Are my eyes and mind focused on the things I can control? Or am I continuously looking at what others in my home are doing wrong?
- How much time do I spend thinking about my former spouse or my partner's previous partner?

Don't be discouraged. God understands. You have not failed. You are learning a new way. And God wants it for you more than you want it for yourself.

PRAYER

"Lord, help me. This study is stirring emotions and feelings in me that I wasn't prepared to tackle. I wasn't ready. I'm starting to feel like I made a big mistake getting into this marriage. If I'm being honest, I'm trying to figure a

way out of it. My spouse would be very hurt right now if he/she knew how badly I'm fighting to stay married. I feel like such a failure.

These stepfamily problems are causing me to belittle, discredit, and turn away from my spouse. I don't want to do that, but my emotions are overwhelming. I feel so discounted, neglected, and disrespected. God, I need your help.

Lord, I dislike my spouse's kids. There I said it out loud—to you. Help me. You can teach me how to love those I dislike. I'm taking my anger towards my spouse out on innocent kids. It's not their fault they are entitled and spoiled. They were taught this.

It doesn't mean I will love them the same as my own family, but you can teach me how to love in any circumstance. Help me to set boundaries with my spouse in a loving way that reveals I won't be disrespected anymore.

And help me to do this out of love, not hate. Not revenge. Not retaliation.

In my own strength I do not have the power. I know it full well.

I need you.

Thank you, Jesus.

~ 3 ~

Overcoming Despair

Elkanah, Hannah, and Peninnah

Even though this family struggles with situations similar to the other families we have discussed, I have included them because they bring additional dynamics and sentiments into stepfamily dynamics.

Hannah, as with the other women we have studied, struggled with infertility. She's one more woman whose bareness was a social embarrassment, not only for her but for her husband. In that day, Elkanah would have had the biblical and cultural permission to leave his wife and divorce her. Instead, we read that he remained lovingly devoted despite the social criticism and his rights under civil law.

> *Because the Lord had closed Hannah's womb, her rival kept provoking her in order to irritate her. This went on year after year. Whenever Hannah went up to the house of the* Lord, *her rival provoked her till she wept and would not eat.* 1 Samuel 1:6-7

To add insult to injury, the other wife, Peninnah, the fertile one, was able to provide her husband with many children. This woman, her adversary, the one who had all the things that Hannah desired, consistently hurled insults at her. This was much more than being a bully. It was relentless, remorseless, unrelenting torture. Scripture clearly exposes the scathing "mean girl" behavior as ruthless and mortifying. It went on for years and years.

To understand the full impact of Hannah's despair, it's crucial to grasp the totality of her humiliation and the vindictiveness she endured for a long time. Her ongoing mortification resulted in bitterness and depression.

Fortunately, Hannah's husband is a loving and compassionate man. He gives her more than he does to his other wife and kids.

> *Whenever the day came for Elkanah to sacrifice, he would give portions of the meat to his wife Peninnah and to all her sons and daughters. But to Hannah he gave a double portion because he loved her, and the LORD had closed her womb.* I Samuel 1:4-5

However, his kindness doesn't change the fact that she had a big problem that her devoted husband could not solve. And he becomes defensive when his acts of kindness aren't enough. He wants to know why his love and favoritism towards her aren't meeting and filling her needs.

> *Her husband Elkanah would say to her, "Hannah, why are you weeping? Why don't you eat? Why are you downhearted? Don't I mean more to you than ten sons?"* 1 Samuel 1:8

This situation often parallels the infertility issues faced by many women today. Men wonder why his kids, created in another woman's womb, are not enough for his wife.

"My kids love my wife, Denise. She's a wonderful stepmom, and they think she's great. Sure, we have normal blending problems, but that's to be expected, "Dave explained. "I don't understand why we need more kids. Denise is obsessed with having a child. We already have kids. I don't want to start all over again with a baby, bottles, formula, and diapers. It just doesn't make sense when you factor in the cost of adding another child. Now that the kids are older and can take care of themselves a little more, we can do what we want. I want to give Denise what she wants, but I just don't get it."

He's right. He doesn't get it.

He has kids. She doesn't.

He views his kids as also being hers. Denise knows these are kids her husband, the love of her life, had with another woman. These children came from another woman's body, a love he had before her. He wants his wife to view his kids as her own. But the mother of those children is the one who got to experience all the baby stuff with him. The delivery room, the excitement, the first steps, and everything involved with bringing a new life into the world.

During Hannah's agony, she begins bargaining with God. Don't we all?

She begs Him to see her misery. She pleads for relief. Then she negotiates with a momentous and bold promise to God. If He gives her a son, she will offer his life back to God's service for all the days of his life. Courageous. Desperate.

Hannah is in such deep lament and intimate communion with the living God that the nearby priest, Eli, thinks she's drunk.

*As she kept on praying to the L*ORD*, Eli observed her mouth. Hannah was praying in her heart, and her lips were* *moving but her voice was not heard. Eli thought she was drunk and said to her, "How long are you going to stay drunk? Put away your wine."* 1 Samuel 1:12-14

Have you ever grieved like that?
I have.
Your soul cries are deep and guttural. It's existing. You must remind yourself to breathe. Bellowing your cry is all you possess. It's all that's left of your body, mind, and soul.
It's hard to describe unless you have lived it.
Hannah is so immersed in her prayer and God's presence that the priest chastises her. She explains what is truly happening,

"Not so, my lord," Hannah replied, "I am a woman who is deeply troubled. I have not been drinking wine or beer; I was pouring out my soul to the Lord. *Do not take your servant for a wicked woman; I have been praying here out of my great anguish and grief." Eli answered, "Go in peace, and may the God of Israel grant you what you have asked of him."* 1 Samuel 1:15-17

Eli realizes he's wrong and then blesses her. And after the prayer and benediction, she walks away a different woman.
Have her circumstances changed? Is she immediately pregnant? NO.
Her soul is resurrected. She eats. Her face changes.
It's significant to note that she was at peace before she was pregnant.
Is her renewed vigor because she proclaimed a "name it and claim it prayer?" The ones often taught and touted

in today's Church. Just tell God what you want, and He will do it. He's obligated to do it. He's at your command to do it. The louder and flashier you shout, the higher your hands are raised, and the fiercer your cry, the better.

God will do it because you prayed it into being.

No, that's not faith. That's ego. That's false religion.

That teaching, which destroys so many baby Christians, is teaching how God must do—will do, is obligated to do—what I ask, in the way that I ask, in the timing I desire.

Notice the number of "I's" in that way of thinking. Which is why it is dangerous and detrimental to our faith.

God is not obligated to answer my prayers. He isn't my slave or a genie in a bottle. He doesn't respond to my commands.

He is God. I am not.

Good thing.

Hannah is at peace because she trusts God with the outcome before she knows the answer. This is faith.

God does what is best, holy, and beneficial. My motives are typically self-focused.

Even if God doesn't do what I request, He is still God.

In Hannah's case, it turns out as she requested. Samuel was born.

Overcoming Despair

Your need to overcome hopelessness might not be due to infertility. There is a plethora of other reasons a person living in a stepfamily can experience despair. The rationale and situations may not be the same as Hannah's, but the solution is.

How did Hannah conquer her despair?

- **Surrender**

    When you finally come to the place where you accept and admit you can't control the circumstances, there is a flood of surrender. The yield is exhausting, and liberation knotted together. Your mind finally releases and relents to the truth. Our humanness longs to be in control to the degree where we possess the false notion that if I just pray more intently, try harder, and become stronger, I can make this thing happen. It's not true. It's a lie. Surrender to the truth.

- **Accept**

    There is not one person, place, or thing I can't lose within the next 20 seconds. I am not in control of everything. Therefore, the next step is to accede and let go. I must accept my limitations and abilities.

- **Discover**

    Next is learning what my part should be in this situation. I can't control all of it; God can. However, there are a few things I can control. What are they? I'm able to manage my thoughts and actions. Good and bad. What thoughts and actions will I decide upon?

- **Ask**

    During Hannah's prayer, we see that she has a shift. Something came upon her during that intense state of prayer which caused her to have hope. I believe it was evidence of the Holy Spirit. I've had it happen to me, so I know it's true. Once you choose to hear God's thoughts instead of your own, it allows Him to provide you with truth. I typically pray, "Lord, give me the mind of Christ. Replace my thoughts with your perspective, wisdom, and truth." He has never failed.

- **Others**

    God provided Eli amid Hannah's predicament. He sometimes uses people to boost our faith and strengthen our belief. Eli provides Hannah with a blessing that encourages her. God created us for community. We need people. He knows it's crucial for us to have a Christian circle. They provide the wisdom, strength, and reinforcement we often need when in a season of despair.

- **Move**

    Hannah walks away from Eli. She doesn't stay there and commiserate. She doesn't go on Facebook and vent. She doesn't seek pity from her friends. She moves. She leaves the temple and takes steps forward. Her face is brighter because she's walking in faith, not despair. Sometimes, we need to change our setting to see things from a different perspective. Nature is always a good place to start. We were created to live in a garden. The Garden. Nature often provides peace and a breath of fresh air.

- **Trust**

    It's easy to tell people to trust God. It's much harder to do it when the world is falling apart. I used to work for author, speaker, and Christian extraordinaire Larry Burkett. When he got kidney cell carcinoma, he said, "If I can just get over the fear, I'll be ok. Do I trust God, or do I just say I trust God?" Trusting God isn't a one-and-done. It's a daily choice to lay myself at the foot of the cross and tell Him, "I believe in you. You are a virtuous God. And I trust you to do what is holy, perfect, and good even if I don't like it."

The Childless/ Childfree Stepmom

I've included a section on adding an "ours" baby to the blended family in this resource. I also want to address the woman who either cannot or doesn't want to add children to the blend. When I began in stepfamily ministry, I assumed my situation of being a childless stepmom, a woman without biological children, was rare. I was wrong.

Some of my sisters desire to add a baby but physically cannot. Many have a husband who had a vasectomy during his first marriage. That was my situation. Others chose not to add a child for various reasons.

I grew up in a stepfamily. My dad married twice after the divorce from my mom. I lived it. I also had a painful childhood, and at an early age, I decided I didn't want to bring children into this painful world. This way of thinking is not at all uncommon for kids of divorce. They either want a big family to surround themselves with love, or, like me, they don't want any children. It's not that I didn't think I'd be a good mom; I wasn't afraid to be a mother. I didn't want to bring a child into a painful world. As a young adult, I hadn't done the work yet to heal my childhood anguish. Therefore, even though my husband was willing to have surgery to reverse the vasectomy, we chose not to move forward.

I also didn't want my stepsons to deal with adding another baby. Not everyone feels this way, and that's wonderful. I'm not saying people shouldn't add a baby to the blend. If you are considering another baby, there is an entire chapter in <u>The Smart Stepmom </u>with insight on how, when, why/why not, etc. In this resource, I've included an with your perspective, wisdom, and truth." He has never failed.

- **Others**

    God provided Eli amid Hannah's predicament. He sometimes uses people to boost our faith and strengthen our belief. Eli provides Hannah with a blessing that encourages her. God created us for community. We need people. He knows it's crucial for us to have a Christian circle. They provide the wisdom, strength, and reinforcement we often need when in a season of despair.

- **Move**

    Hannah walks away from Eli. She doesn't stay there and commiserate. She doesn't go on Facebook and vent. She doesn't seek pity from her friends. She moves. She leaves the temple and takes steps forward. Her face is brighter because she's walking in faith, not despair. Sometimes, we need to change our setting to see things from a different perspective. Nature is always a good place to start. We were created to live in a garden. The Garden. Nature often provides peace and a breath of fresh air.

- **Trust**

    It's easy to tell people to trust God. It's much harder to do it when the world is falling apart. I used to work for author, speaker, and Christian extraordinaire Larry Burkett. When he got kidney cell carcinoma, he said, "If I can just get over the fear, I'll be ok. Do I trust God, or do I just say I trust God?" Trusting God isn't a one-and-done. It's a daily choice to lay myself at the foot of the cross and tell Him, "I believe in you. You are a virtuous God. And I trust you to do what is holy, perfect, and good even if I don't like it."

The Childless/ Childfree Stepmom

I've included a section on adding an "ours" baby to the blended family in this resource. I also want to address the woman who either cannot or doesn't want to add children to the blend. When I began in stepfamily ministry, I assumed my situation of being a childless stepmom, a woman without biological children, was rare. I was wrong.

Some of my sisters desire to add a baby but physically cannot. Many have a husband who had a vasectomy during his first marriage. That was my situation. Others chose not to add a child for various reasons.

I grew up in a stepfamily. My dad married twice after the divorce from my mom. I lived it. I also had a painful childhood, and at an early age, I decided I didn't want to bring children into this painful world. This way of thinking is not at all uncommon for kids of divorce. They either want a big family to surround themselves with love, or, like me, they don't want any children. It's not that I didn't think I'd be a good mom; I wasn't afraid to be a mother. I didn't want to bring a child into a painful world. As a young adult, I hadn't done the work yet to heal my childhood anguish. Therefore, even though my husband was willing to have surgery to reverse the vasectomy, we chose not to move forward.

I also didn't want my stepsons to deal with adding another baby. Not everyone feels this way, and that's wonderful. I'm not saying people shouldn't add a baby to the blend. If you are considering another baby, there is an entire chapter in <u>The Smart Stepmom</u> with insight on how, when, why/why not, etc. In this resource, I've included an appendix with suggestions, thoughts, and the effects on the other kids when bringing an ours baby (I'm told the new phrase is a "we" baby) into the family.

What I'm addressing here is women like Sarah and Hannah, who initially did not have a child.

A childless or child-free (the term many use when they choose not to add a baby) stepmom experiences a VERY different journey than a stepmom with her own biological kids.

Here Are Some of the Reasons:

- No one in the home is a blood relative.
- When the blood family naturally squares off into its corner, she's alone.
- She feels like an outsider. They all bonded before she arrived.
- She doesn't fit into "mom" groups at church, neighborhood, etc.
- People tell her she's not a "real mom" even if she has taken on the role with the stepkids full time.
- The husband shares a life-changing experience with his ex-wife that he doesn't have with her.
- A fear of the future. Without biological kids, who will take care of this woman when she's old?
- Extended family treats her like a stranger because there is no child connection to make them related.
- Pets become like children to her. They love her unconditionally.
- She misses her own biological family. Holidays are often spent feeling alone with strangers.
- A bond to biological nieces and nephews that is strong.
- Fear of financial devastation when the husband dies.

- Loneliness is greater with no biological child to focus upon.
- When she dies, there won't be anyone to carry her legacy.

Not all childless stepmoms experience these situations. However, many do or will.

The crucial step for a childless stepmom is to have a circle of friends, including stepmom sisters. This will be her lifeline. They become family. If she has a healthy biological family, they can be a great support if they live nearby. If family isn't nearby, many childless stepmoms share how they desperately miss their nieces and nephews, which feel more like family than her stepkids.

I have a Zoom with Greg Pettys on stepfamily finances on my website. He is the co-author of the book *The Smart Stepfamily Guide to Financial Planning*. It is imperative for a childless stepmom and her spouse to discover the ways she can be prepared and protected. I highly recommend watching the Zoom and receiving the free offer from Greg for one FREE private session for anyone who obtains the Zoom.

I personally don't regret the choice not to have children. I believe God had and still has a different call on my life. That said, it doesn't mean I don't struggle. I must consistently remember that God is my Provider. My husband, his kids, his grandkids, and my biological family are not my source of money, safety, or strength. Almighty God is my only consistent Supplier.

WHAT DO WE LEARN FROM THIS STEPFAMILY?

- Despair is normal
- Bullies have existed since time began

- It's possible to remain godly when being attacked.
- Sometimes, the wicked seem to flourish more than the godly
- Some husbands in the OT showed compassion towards women
- It can take years for God to answer our prayers
- Church leaders can misunderstand our passion for God
- Pray relentlessly

HOW DOES LEARNING ABOUT *THIS* STEPFAMILY STRENGTHEN *MY* STEPFAMILY?

- Elkanah is an excellent role model for a spouse. His compassion and faithfulness to her despite her desperation are to be commended.
- We must be careful not to deprive the former family to "feed" the new wife. A remarriage and more kids don't grant permission to abandon the responsibility to provide for the first set of children. 1 Timothy 5:8 clearly explains this: "Anyone who does not provide for their relatives, and especially for their own household, has denied the faith and is worse than an unbeliever."
- Sometimes, it can feel like God is taking a vacation from our prayers. This stepfamily reveals He hears. He sees. God knows your stepfamily struggles. He hasn't abandoned you.
- At first, Eli didn't get it. Many stepfamilies express this same sentiment when they attempt to explain the unique and complex blended family dynamics to their church or pastor. However, once Hannah clearly

explained, he offered her a blessing. Don't give up. Help your church create a ministry for stepfamilies.
- We don't know how Hannah responded to the harassing wife. We do know it didn't paralyze her or send her into such a fury that she couldn't move forward. Are you allowing the other home to dictate your next steps? Prayers? Dreams? If so, why have you given so much power and brain space to the other home?

PRAYER

Holy God, I admit, I'm in despair. I frequently don't know what to do or where to turn. I'm desperate for you.

When life seems bleak and I don't know where to turn, you are my hope.

Thank you, God, for never leaving me.

Please help me to accept your answers even when I don't like them. Help me trust that you know more than I do, and when I'm in the waiting room or get a no, you are still a good God.

Jesus, these things I'm praying for are hard to live. Give me your strength. I lay down my weakness and exchange it for your power.

Teach me to trust that you know what you are doing. And you will never withhold something that is good and best for me.

Take me deeper in my connection to you during this trial and season of despair. Show me where to seek hope, like Hannah did. Teach me to let go of doing things my way and surrender to your divine way.

My humanness can't, but your holiness can.

I love you, Lord. I trust you, even when I can't see. Amen.

~ 4 ~

Overcoming Bitterness

Joseph Part 1 - Siblings, Stepsiblings, and Half-Siblings

"Laura, since stepfamilies aren't mentioned in Scripture, I'd like to know what Bible reference you would like to use for our broadcast today?"

Attempting to hide my surprise at the radio host's question–and not wanting to sound flippant–I replied, "Well, maybe we should start with Joseph. He was a stepdad—to Jesus."

Long. Pause.

"Wow! You're right. I never thought of that before," he responded.

His reply isn't uncommon. I meet many people who have never considered how the Bible, in particular the Old Testament, is jam-packed with stepfamilies. Part of my job is educating the church and church leaders on blending families and how they are different, with different needs, than first-time families.

The Bible is one of the most profound resources for cultivating, developing, and enriching the people of Jesus

Christ on the knowledge of stepfamily dynamics. We are enlightened and tutored when we study the stepfamilies who walked this same earth many years ago.

Maybe you have encountered Christian leaders who don't understand or embrace blended or stepfamilies.

Don't let it bother you. It's normal.

As we have explored already, the customs and cultures of our Old Testament brothers and sisters are different from today's stepfamily. However, the fears, fights, emotions, loneliness, and complexities are frequently the same. Jealousy, anger, rejection, resentment, stepsibling rivalry, and children who don't know where to place their allegiance are a familiar setting.

Never is this truer than in the story of Joseph, but the son of Jacob, and the grandson of Abraham.

Some half-siblings get along well, and others do not.

The story of Joseph's family begins with his dad, Jacob, and his mom Rachel, who is described as the one Jacob loved. There are many half-siblings and a biological baby brother. Jacob, his wives, and his stepfamily reveal a troubled and dreadful home life. They didn't live in perfect harmony. The dynamics of how they formed a blended family set them up for disaster. The foundation of this family is built upon generational anger, resentment, sorrow, and rejection.

Hopefully, this brings some encouragement as we recognize that even those from the Old Testament who are admirable made poor choices.

With Abraham as his grandpa, the extensive sibling rivalry, hatred, and suffering they experienced was all due to family members who chose to disobey God. They went their own way with disastrous consequences. Therefore, it's crucial to learn about these families. They are an excellent reminder of what happens when we choose to step outside of God's wisdom and protection.

The sin done to us can often lead to the sin done by us.

And the kids are duplicating what they have witnessed.

The good news is this family has a happy ending. And God reveals how any stepfamily can find peace and reconciliation if the correct choices and effort are taken.

Our past does not own the future. The choices of our ancestors, good or bad, do not need to dictate or have authority over our life. God's specialty is rescuing, redeeming, resurrecting, and restoring. He makes all things new. Joseph's life reveals how God can take the most dysfunctional stepfamily and turn things around for good. This should provide hope and assurance that God is capable and willing to do for us what He did for them. He is the same God.

Jesus Christ is the same yesterday and today and forever.
Hebrews 13:8

Perhaps the greatest part of this stepfamily story is how God took this pathetic, jumbled, contorted, destructive mess—and used it. He repairs the ugly, jealous, sinful actions of some and turns the entire scenario around, using it for good and His glory.

The key verses are found here. They explain how the problems began for poor old Joe.

Now Israel (aka Jacob) loved Joseph more than any of his other sons, because he had been born to him in his old age; and he made an ornate robe for him. When his brothers

saw that their father loved him more than any of them, they hated him and could not speak a kind word to him.
Genesis 37:3-4

YIKES!

The essence of this family's problem arises from Jacob. The extreme favoritism he lavishes on Joseph, the "ours" baby, with his beloved Rachel, creates a hurricane of adverse reactions in the other kids. Even though young Joey is a bit cocky, he isn't the root problem. This son is simply reacting to how he has been raised.

This is a common problem in stepfamilies. And the stepparent (usually a stepmom) frequently labels the spouse's biological child as being a self-centered little brat who picks on her "ours" child.

The truth is the stepchild is merely acting out as they have been taught.

Who is primarily to blame for Joseph's taunting attitude? Dear old Dad!

And one day, the older half-brothers decide they have had enough of dad's favoritism. They retaliate in a most horrific way. They detest and loathe Joseph, and their profound animosity forms into a devious plot to get rid of their baby half-brother—forever.

But they saw him in the distance, and before he reached them, they plotted to kill him.

"Here comes that dreamer!" they said to each other. "Come now, let's kill him and throw him into one of these cisterns and say that a ferocious animal devoured him. Then we'll see what comes of his dreams. When Reuben heard this, he tried to rescue him from their hands. "Let's not take his life," he said. "Don't shed any

blood. Throw him into this cistern here in the wilderness, but don't lay a hand on him." Reuben said this to rescue him from them and take him back to his father.
Genesis 37:18-21

Only his half-brother, Reuben, fears the sin of murdering his brother. And he talks the other brothers into throwing him into a pit instead.

Then Judah, another half-brother, has the brilliant idea of playing "Let's Make a Deal" by selling him into slavery rather than letting him rot. He decides it's wise to make some cash out of the situation, which sweetens the pot of Joseph's disappearance.

Joseph is sold into slavery. It appears all his dreams were nothing more than an illusion.

Or were they?

Joseph's master took him and put him in prison, the place where the king's prisoners were confined.

But while Joseph was there in the prison, the LORD was with him; he showed him kindness and granted him favor in the eyes of the prison warden. So, the warden put Joseph in charge of all those held in the prison, and he was made responsible for all that was done there. The warden paid no attention to anything under Joseph's care, because the LORD was with Joseph and gave him success in whatever he did.
Genesis 39: 20-23

Joseph was born into a family characterized by great brokenness and sadness. Lying, jealousy, secrecy, and betrayal were the foundations for his life. He spent 10-13 years in prison, completely cut off from his family. God never discards any of our past for his future when we surrender ourselves to him. Every mistake and choice we make in the journey of life is used by God.

The Why Behind the Pain?

"Why did God allow Joseph to go through such pain and loss? We see traces of the good that came out of it in Genesis 37 through 50, but much remains a mystery. Most important for us to recognize today is that Joseph did not deny his past but trusted in God's goodness and love, even when circumstances went from bad to worse.[4]

While in prison, God's hand and blessings are upon Joseph. The bratty little ours baby brother, who was despised by his half-brothers, turns out to be a very godly man.

In chapters Genesis 40-42, the entire story unravels as we watch Papa Jacob deeply grieve the loss of his favored son. He continues to inflict shame and humiliation on his other sons, except for the other ours baby Benjamin. Even in his tremendous sorrow, he displays to the other sons that Joseph and Ben are the only sons that matter to him.

As the situation intensifies, disaster strikes. A famine hits the land. Jacob and his family are desperate. They need food or they will die.

> *When Jacob learned that there was grain in Egypt, he said to his sons, "Why do you just keep looking at each other?" He continued, "I have heard that there is grain in Egypt. Go down there and buy some for us, so that we may live and not die."*
>
> *Then ten of Joseph's brothers went down to buy grain from Egypt. But Jacob did not send Benjamin, Joseph's*

---

4 Emotionally Healthy Spirituality, Peter Scazzero, 2017 (Grand Rapids MI) p111-115

brother, with the others, because he was afraid that harm might come to him. So Israel's sons were among those who went to buy grain, for there was famine in the land of Canaan also. Genesis 42:1-5

Jacob discovers there is grain in a city far away. He doesn't know it's where his own son, Joseph, resides.

But Joseph isn't in prison anymore. On no! God allowed some terrible circumstances to occur to Joseph for the sole purpose of strengthening him and testing his integrity. And God eventually raised up this son and allowed him to become a ruler. He's now in charge of the food Jacob and the other family members need to survive.

The brothers ask for the grain, but they don't recognize little brother Joey. He's a man now. He looks different, acts different, and talks differently.

He's dressed as a prominent leader. I envision a fashionista with black kohl eyeliner; Egyptians are known for that fashion statement. His clothing would have been lavish and likely constructed with gold embellishments.

To add to their conundrum, Joseph is now speaking a different language. He can understand them because they are communicating in his native tongue. However, they can't converse with him. And they assume he doesn't understand what they are saying.

> *"They did not realize that Joseph could understand them, since he was using an interpreter."* Genesis 42:23

Joseph sets up many requirements he demands to prove they are worthy of obtaining the grain. One stipulation is that they must leave one brother there with Joseph, then return with the youngest brother, Benjamin.

We must remember this is Joseph's only full blood sibling.

Don't miss the message of blood connection. Don't despise the blood relationship. There is something in us that has a supernatural and profound connection to people with our DNA. God created it.

When stepfamily members become resentful because there is a closer and tighter bond with those who are blood relatives, it sets them up for pain. It's normal. Our society attempts to push "there are no steps in this family" so hard that it causes a hindrance when someone is more attached or committed to a blood relative.

Why? Why do we think less of a stepchild, grandparent, or aunt who feels closer to their own family member than they do to a new family member? This doesn't give permission to the relative for acting out in abuse, neglect, or dismissal. But the notion that everyone is happy about the "insta-family" creates tremendous stress and pain for everyone.

I love to watch television shows where a long-lost son or daughter is reunited with a biological parent who gave them up for adoption. I cry every time they first see each other.

Why?

Because family is different. I grew up in a big Italian family, and my grandparents were immigrants to the USA. My nana would repeatedly say to us, "That's your family, that's your blood. You don't ever walk away from family. You take care of family."

Is it any wonder I have codependency issues? However, that's for another book.

Those of us in stepfamilies have created a circle of shame around the truth. We must stop despising and minimizing the fact that our kids have a supernatural bond with those that share the same DNA. Even if those people do not treat them well or abandon them.

In our effort to lovingly blend, we have erased God's supernatural connection with biological family. We criticize and ridicule kids who don't desire or bond with stepsiblings. Because we adults want them to function as a nuclear family, we chastise the kids and the stepparent for not having the same feelings. It's wrong. Because it's natural, and designed by God, to feel closer and have a desire for those in our own family.

That doesn't give permission to be rude, calloused, hurtful, or ostracizing to stepfamily members. It does extend grace and forgiveness when they gravitate to their own blood.

Now, let's go back to Joseph.

Joseph's stepbrothers beg him to reconsider. He remains steadfast.

Now, the brothers have the dreaded task of going home and telling their dad that unless the other favored son, Benjamin, goes back with them, the brother who was left with the grain owner is gone. And the king won't give them the food they need to survive.

They are in one hot mess.

Jacob won't have any of it.

> *But Jacob said, "My son will not go down there with you; his brother is dead, and he is the only one left. If harm comes to him on the journey you are taking, you will bring my gray head down to the grave in sorrow."* Genesis: 42:38

In modern language, "over my dead body."

Wow! As if they haven't been humiliated and chastened enough, daddy's words hit below the belt this time. If the older sons ever questioned whether Jacob truly does favor Joseph and Benjamin, this seals the deal.

Jacob's lament causes him to spew these annihilating words, "He is the only son I have left."

Imagine what the brothers are thinking. Do you hear them proclaiming, "Wow! He really does hate us!"

Jacob's words are an emotional, all-consuming stab to the heart.

The guilty sons are left in shame and sorrow as they absorb what they have done. The entire family might die because of their sin.

And dad's brutal words reveal they are:

- Degraded. Our father doesn't trust us anymore.
- Disgraced. We killed our brother; this is our fault.
- Discredited. Dad doesn't even consider me a son anymore.
- Desperate. Dad, go ahead and kill my own sons if I don't do it right this time.
- Dismayed. If Benjamin doesn't go, it's all over.
- Dishonored. The sorrow we have caused our dad is killing him.
- Destroyed. If we're unable to get food, we will all die.
- Disbelief. Who would have ever dreamed it could get this bad?

This is what sin creates. This is why God hates it. This is why God tells us not to act out with lies, manipulation, revenge, jealousy, anger, resentment, and unforgiveness.

If, from the beginning, Laban hadn't deceived Jacob, he would have married the right woman, the woman he loved in the first place. If Jacob hadn't cultivated and nurtured bitterness toward his father-in-law, he wouldn't have favored Joseph over his other children. Because of their father's atrocious attitude, these sons learned it was acceptable to respond to jealousy with anger and bitterness.

Jacob taught his sons that it was good to seek revenge. This bird's eye view has shown them it is acceptable to take matters into their own hands and retaliate against the brother who gets all of dad's love and attention.

This is called a generational curse.

It is the sinful behavior practiced by one generation, observed, and repeated in the next generation. It is initiated by Satan. He loves it and uses it often. And if it goes unchecked and unhealed by God, the curse can continue for many years.

The goal is always the same: to annihilate the family emotionally, spiritually, mentally, and physically.

But it doesn't have to be that way.

I have a family history of certain generational curses. Not murder, but alcohol and some other damaging stuff. I recently read a statement that rang true for me. "It ran in the family—until it ran into me."

Even though those family plagues stopped with me, it doesn't mean I don't still battle the consequences. Discovering how those wounds still can play out in our current lives is crucial.

In her resource Making Peace and Beyond, Jamie Norton taught me why. "When a child is violated, devalued, shamed, or humiliated, they must learn to survive in a world that is unsafe, abusive, chaotic, and unpredictable. They learn to speak the 'language of survival' as their first language. The language of survival is a reactive language. It is spoken in an attempt to self-protect in an environment that is perceived to be dangerous. One does not stop speaking their first language simply because they leave home." [5]

I chose to follow Christ instead of allowing the pattern to continue. And with that came the Holy Spirit's power, strength, and ability to change. I asked God to teach me how to think and respond in a holy, healthier manner.

And He did.

It wasn't overnight, and it wasn't easy. But He is faithful in continuing to heal me from those things daily. I continue in that process, and sometimes my stepfamily dynamic triggers that old survival language. I'm now aware of what it is and how to turn down the volume.

God is bigger than Satan's attempts to shackle us with evil and darkness. God is always faithful and capable. Your family's past doesn't have to become your future.

Will you be the one to stop a generational sin in your family? Do you believe and recognize that there is no evil powerful enough to overcome the Holy Spirit?

You are not a victim of your circumstances even when it feels that way. You can be victorious. But you must learn how.

We will study the conclusion of Joseph, his brothers, father, and family in the next chapter. For now, dive into what we have read so far and seek God's truth, validating there is never a situation so bleak that He can't redeem it.

WHAT DO WE LEARN FROM THIS STEPFAMILY?

Joseph's life is an excellent illustration of God's character and the lessons we can learn in the dark pit of life.

---

5   Making Peace and Beyond, A Workbook for Change, Jamie Norton Med, LICDC-CS, self-published. MakingPeaceandBeyond.com

- Changes occur when we are in a dark season of life. They don't have to be bad changes.
- God's character and availability never change.
- When God says, "No, don't do that," it really is for our good.
- A parent's behavior and actions are witnessed by his kids. And often repeated.
- Joseph had the ability to remain strong even in the worst setting. God can take us from being the victim to the victor when we trust Him with the results.
- Feeling completely rejected, unloved, and abandoned by your family is normal for people who grew up in unloving and complex circumstances.
- God can override a man's plan to destroy.

HOW DOES LEARNING ABOUT *THIS* STEPFAMILY STRENGTHEN *MY* STEPFAMILY?

Digging deeper into this biblical family can reveal some of the ways parents and stepparents are causing division and resentment in their blended family. Ponder these thoughts.

- What repetitive patterns did you observe in your family growing up (good or bad)? Have you worked to resolve any negative consequences of those patterns?
- What patterns have continued into your family? (good or bad)
- Why is it more common in stepfamilies to have favorites? Can a stepparent love stepkids "just like their own," or is this unrealistic?
- When one child is favored, it naturally creates resentment in the other children. Do I favor one child over another?

- How do we handle gifts? When giving gifts, don't show favoritism. Lavishing one child with gifts and not the others is a breeding ground for anger and bitterness to take root. However, you can't control the gifts given to kids or stepkids from the other home. Therefore, "fair" isn't always possible in a stepfamily.
- It's not uncommon for siblings/stepsiblings/halfsiblings to dislike each other. Parents can't force them to bond; it's unwise to try. However, a parent needs to correct hurtful behaviors. If left unchecked, it can be destructive and dangerous.
- Did I have unrealistic expectations regarding the kids bonding? How can I change that point of view?
- What am I doing as a parent or stepparent that motivates unity between siblings and stepsiblings? Is my attitude toward my stepchild's other parent part of the reason there is discord in our home?

PRAYER

Lord, what a mess we make of things. How do you even tolerate us, much less love us? Thank you for taking the disasters I have created and turning them around for good.

Joseph's family gives me hope. When my own blended family feels like it's fractured and crumbling, you remind me that nothing is too big for you.

Lord, I have a child like Jacob. He/she is mean, resentful, and potentially dangerous. I'm afraid of him/her. I'm concerned he/she could hurt other family members, and I don't know what to do about it. This risky person is testing my patience and my trust in you. My spouse isn't listening, and I feel like I'm the only one willing to admit and address the problem.

I need your wisdom, Lord. Before something worse happens, I need your strength. Tell me what to do, who to speak with, and where to go for help. Speak to me about how to act on the things that are my responsibility and let go of the things I can't control.

When I entered a stepfamily, I never imagined I'd face things this complex. But you knew. And you have already prepared a plan and a way. I'm listening. Send me to a godly person who can help me. I trust you to provide. Amen.

~ 5 ~
OVERCOMING RESENTMENT, FINDING FORGIVENESS

Joseph Part 2 - When Your Family Hurts You

In her Bible study *Finding God Faithful*, Kelly Minter says, "Joseph was born into a complicated family, but that didn't keep God from setting him apart for a great purpose." [6]

This truth should bring us hope.

As we study the conclusion of Joseph's family and the pain created, we discover that God's plans are far superior and more profound than anything we could ever ask or think. He can take the darkest sin and turn it around for good.

God uses the sin done to us, and the sin done by us, for his glory—if we let Him.

Nothing is wasted in His hands.

And now the conclusion of the suspenseful story. What happens when the brothers return to Joseph? Will he become angry that he has been robbed of many years with

---

6 Lifeway Press, Kelly Minter, Finding God Faithful, 2020, Nashville, TN , p9

his father? Will he embrace his full biological baby brother, Benjamin?

We read in Genesis 43 that Benjamin is by their side when the brothers appear again to Joseph. Daddy didn't want to let his youngest one go, but they finally convinced him. It required a solemn vow to protect the adolescent beloved brother.

As the camera zooms in, we see Joseph and the look on his face when he sees his brother for the first time since they were kids. It's been thirteen years. He was a teen when he left, and Benjamin was a child. Does he remember playing together in the safety of their backyard? Is he astonished that his brother is now a young man? Does his brother's broad shoulders and handsome face bring tears of joy? Or is he overwhelmed with grief by the years his brothers stole from him?

We don't know everything, but we do observe his reaction. And it's powerful.

> *"As he looked about and saw his brother Benjamin, his mother's son, he asked, "Is this your youngest brother, the one you told me about?" And he said, "God be gracious to you, my son." Deeply moved at the sight of his brother, Joseph hurried out and looked for a place to weep. He went into his private room and wept there."* Genesis 43:29-30

I can't comprehend the thoughts that consumed Joseph's mind, heart, and soul. We know that he was so overwhelmed with emotion that he had to turn away to hide it from the others. Seeing his baby brother stimulates his pent-up, shoved-down, and buried heartache. It spontaneously seizes his heart to overflowing. He weeps.

In today's words, he had a meltdown—one of those moments when you simply can't contain yourself. No amount of self-talk, prayer, or persuasion can stop the uncontrollable emotions. And the floodgate to his soul erupted.

I don't know if this type of response has ever happened to you, but I have experienced it. A person never forgets it. This uncontrollable assault of feelings leaves us face down on the floor in a puddle of tears. There is no strength, concentration, or desire to do anything else.

Family can hurt us like no one else. They are designed by God to be our safe place to fall and enclose us with people who have our back. Unconditional love and a soft place to lay our head is the original goal of the family.

Often, it's not reality. And when they wound us, especially if it's intentional as it was with Joseph, the laceration runs deep. It assaults our significance and confirms our foulest fear, "I am unloved. I am worthless. I am contemptible."

After time in solitude, Joseph acquires enough self-control to contain his emotions, and he returns to his brothers.

> *"Then after he had washed his face, he came out and, controlling himself, said, 'Serve the food.'"* Genesis 43:31.

He does what any nice Jewish boy would do, he says, "Let's eat!" His mama would be proud.

And then he plays a trick on his brothers. He hides money in Benjamin's backpack and then instructs his servants to intentionally "discover" it. The penalty for thievery is that Benjamin must stay behind with Joseph.

Joseph is a godly man, and we don't know this for sure, but it's possible he intentionally does this to give them a "taste of their own medicine." They plead and beg to release Benjamin and send them back to the dad. They tell Joseph the father will surely die if they return without him.

Emotionally, the man will not make it if Benjamin is missing too.

Soon, he can take no more of watching his brothers writhing in emotional pain. My guess is the look of fear on Benjamin's face did it. True love doesn't enjoy watching a family member suffer, even when they deserve it.

Joseph sends all the servants away. And he cries and reveals himself to the brothers.

> *And he wept so loudly that the Egyptians heard him, and Pharaoh's household heard about it. Joseph said to his brothers, "I am Joseph! Is my father still living?" But his brothers were not able to answer him because they were terrified at his presence. Then Joseph said to his brothers, "Come close to me." When they had done so, he said, "I am your brother Joseph, the one you sold into Egypt! And now, do not be distressed and do not be angry with yourselves for selling me here, because it was to save lives that God sent me ahead of you.* Genesis 45:2-5

The wailing. Oh my gosh, the sounds which came from Joseph were excruciating. Scripture tells us he was bawling so loudly that the entire household heard it, including the Egyptians and Pharaoh's people. This is an extraordinary cry only heard in extreme circumstances. Many describe it as guttural and almost inhumane, almost animal-like. It is a rasping, husky sound that cannot be feigned or contrived. It's coming spontaneously from the bottom of the soul.

And that is where we find Joseph. In a moment of deep release, he finally tells his brothers who he is and where they are. Can you imagine the shock?

And then...

The most incredible thing happens to these men.

He doesn't blame them. He doesn't bash, trash, annihilate, swear, scorn, or retaliate. He doesn't heap shame, revenge, or bitterness upon them. He does just the opposite. He tells them it's okay.

To prove he isn't holding revenge against them, he gives them gifts. And when Pharaoh discovers these are his brothers, he adds more vehicles, gifts, food, and livestock.

Israel (Jacob) has a hard time believing that his son is alive.

> *They told him, "Joseph is still alive! In fact, he is ruler of all Egypt." Jacob was stunned; he did not believe them. But when they told him everything Joseph had said to them, and when he saw the carts, Joseph had sent to carry him back, the spirit of their father Jacob revived. And Israel said, "I'm convinced! My son Joseph is still alive. I will go and see him before I die."* Genesis 45:27-28

This is what forgiveness looks like.

Joseph's family is reunited, his dad is happy, and they end on a very good note.

Be honest. The magnitude of this type of forgiveness seems unrealistic. And that's where God comes in. On his own strength, Joseph couldn't have forgiven them. But he had thirteen years to learn. And in those years, many things happened to teach him. God does not discard our pain. He cultivates it.

> *"God will not waste your pain. God specializes in sowing seeds into the soil of our hardship, seeds that bring forth prolific life and bear fruit in season."* [7]

---

7 Lifeway Press, Kelly Minter, Finding God Faithful, 2020, Nashville, TN , p77

What does forgiveness look like in today's stepfamily?

Angela knew she need to forgive her stepdaughter, Kylie, but she didn't know how.

Kylie had stolen an heirloom bracelet that belonged to Angela's deceased mother. The bracelet was in Angela's jewelry box.

If that wasn't bad enough, Kylie lied and denied taking it. Six months later, Angela was cleaning Kylie's messy bedroom and found it hidden. When she showed the bracelet to her husband and demanded that he reprimand Kylie, he became very quiet. Later, he said he'd talk with his daughter about it. Angela knew what that meant. She had been here before. It would go the same way as the last time her stepdaughter stole something of hers.

Nothing would be done about it—again. Angela's husband would threaten Kylie with a punishment and never follow through. So, it happened again and again.

The bitterness was consuming Angela. She wanted to overcome the anger and resentment but couldn't let it go no matter how hard she tried.

Forgiving someone can be one of the hardest things to do, especially if the person lives in your home. And if they aren't sorry for what they did, like Kylie, it's even worse.

Most Christians understand the importance of forgiveness; they know the teachings of Jesus. We comprehend that Jesus teaches us to forgive. However, very little has been taught how.

And this lack of how, the practical steps, is a common reason why a Christian will harbor the endless cycle of bitterness and revenge. He or she has an inaccurate, perverted, or distorted view of forgiveness.

Christian resources explain the benefits of forgiveness, but defining and embracing what forgiveness is, and is not, is often the key to success.

This goes double for the stepfamily because the relationships are not organic, like a biological family. The bonds are different and often complex. Emotions run high.

Blended families are somewhat bonded to each other because of a remarriage, but they are not related to each other in many ways. The marriage came after the kids were born to another couple. Forgiveness in this awkward, perplexing dynamic can become a confusing mess of reactions.

This is why understanding how to forgive those in our stepfamily requires a bit more depth and exploration.

Let's look at Angela's scenario. Who is the object of her anger?

Kylie? Yes, the child stole.

Her husband? Yes, because he should be holding his daughter accountable.

Her marriage? Yes, she didn't realize the remarriage would cause her to live in a home where her things must consistently be under lock and key.

Herself? Yes, she often blames herself for putting her biological daughter in a home that isn't safe and free from burglary. Angela now views herself as "a terrible mother," which was not her viewpoint before the remarriage.

God? Yes. She wonders why God didn't warn her that remarriage and stepfamily life would be like this.

And then Satan baits her with a dagger of doubt about the relationship and whispers, "Maybe you should leave this marriage."

Learning how to forgive is a vital part of keeping any family intact. And we will start with what forgiveness is NOT.

Forgiveness is not a feeling.
If Angela waits until she feels like forgiving Maddie, it's unlikely to occur. God knows that hanging on to revenge, anger, and rage can destroy us spiritually, emotionally, and physically. Christ paid too much for us to be a slave to anything, much less hatred. He wants his children free. And a person is never free when weighed down with the ball and chain of bitterness. When the cold shackles of revenge are tightly clasped around our wrists, it's impossible to lift our hands to praise Him. Therefore, the initial steps toward forgiveness are an act of obedience to God because we trust him and believe he has our best interest at heart. He wants us healed more than we do.

Forgiveness is not pretending you were not hurt.
Depicting a phony plastic smile when you are emotionally dying inside is not forgiveness. In Scripture, we never see Jesus "Fake it till you make it." When he is sad, he cries (John 11:35). When he is angry, he turns over the tables in the temple (John 2:15-16). When he is lonely, he cries to his Daddy (Matthew 26:39). Christianity is not about denying a wound or living a charade. Maddie has betrayed Angela's trust. A loss has occurred. She is justified in acknowledging and declaring the hurt instigated by Maddie's sinful and poor choice.

Forgiveness is not saying what the person did is acceptable.
Many people reject forgiving another because it feels as though the wrongdoer is getting away with the offense. And in stepfamilies, if the parent doesn't hold the child accountable, the problem gets worse.

Our human nature wants the person who hurt us to suffer, as we have. Forgiveness isn't ignoring what the person did or pretending they are a good person. It is possible to acknowledge the wound and identify the person who caused it without letting the offense embed bitterness.

If Maddie were Angela's own child, she would have the bond and parental authority to implement a consequence. However, a stepparent has a radically different relationship from a parent. The trust, emotions, and heartfelt dynamics are entirely different. Therefore, the biological parent MUST be the one.

Forgiveness is not trusting the person.

Forgiveness does not mean you immediately allow the person back into your life or your heart. After a betrayal, if the relationship is to be restored, it is crucial for the offender to establish trust. This takes time. The depth of the offense often dictates what needs to be done.

Trust is not an offender's automatic right. If a person is remorseful and willing to do the hard work necessary to restore the relationship, trust can eventually be authenticated. Repentance is humble—not demanding. A contrite person doesn't make demands, manipulate Bible verses, or blame others.

Some people shouldn't be trusted. Right now, Kylie falls into this category because she has stolen at least twice and continues to show no remorse. And a stepchild often doesn't feel the need to repent to the stepparent because they don't care if the relationship is broken. However, a biological connection is different.

Forgiveness is not relieving the person of responsibility.

A person shouldn't be "off the hook" from his or her responsibilities because of forgiveness.

Forgiveness doesn't eradicate responsibility. It's not unloving to hold someone accountable. It's often the most loving thing you can do because without a consequence, many never feel the pain of their actions. Dad must require Kylie to return the bracelet or replace it if it's been damaged.

Forgiveness is not always a one-time event.
Those closest to us may hurt us repeatedly, like Kylie has done. That doesn't eliminate the command from God to forgive. It does tell us that she is unsafe. Angela may need to learn how to forgive her multiple times, but that doesn't mean she should trust her or leave jewelry lying on a dresser.

And this is where the stepfamily dynamic becomes a hot problem. Angela feels her home should be her safe space, not a place where she must keep things under lock and key. But dad may be afraid to pressure his daughter too much, fearing she won't return to visit him again. It's likely the reason he hasn't implemented tougher boundaries before now. He's in a very delicate and complex dynamic.

Angela will need to pray over her list of those she's angry with before healing can take place. And she and her husband will have to have hard conversations free from shame, yelling, accusations, warnings, and demanding threats.

Angela has every right to feel wounded, victimized, angry, and alone in this situation. However, unforgiveness towards Kylie won't make it better. You can forgive and still love someone yet refrain from trusting them again. Especially when it's a child.

God is more than willing to teach us how to surrender every hurt and rejection to him so that it produces wholeness. And that often begins with discovering the difference between what forgiveness is and what it is not.

Joseph's brothers didn't apologize, and they couldn't give him back the years they took from him. And yet Joseph found a way to look at the big picture instead of wallowing in bitterness.

I had, and sometimes still have, to make similar choices with my biological family and my stepfamily.

It is not easy. It is not immediate. It is not a one-time occurrence.

It is liberating.

Releasing the results to God and trusting him with the results brings tremendous relief.

If Angela wants to find peace, she will need to let go of the need to prove to her spouse that his daughter is a thief. Deep down, he knows.

She will need to accept that placing her personal items in a locked space is the only solution right now and pray that Kylie gets the help she needs to stop. She will need to ask God to help her see Kylie through His eyes, not her angry eyes. She will need to forgive her.

And it's likely it will be more than once. Why? Because it's family.

Angela may need to put emotional distance between her and her stepdaughter until her heart heals. It's okay to take time to heal.

CAUTION: Work to keep the pain from creating resentment that leads to animosity, scorn, and a hard heart.

God's Perspective

Does God expect us to forgive someone who isn't repentant? Yes. Does God expect us to forgive someone who doesn't ask for forgiveness? Yes. Does God expect us to have a relationship with that person? Not necessarily. Each situation is different.

Forgiveness, trust, and reconciliation are entirely different things. After a betrayal, trust must be earned over time.

I can forgive someone and not have a relationship with them. I can absolve and not be reunited.

If I ask God, He will teach me the difference between holding onto an offense as a form of revenge due to a hard heart or whether I'm keeping someone at arm's length (or out of my life) because it's wise. Often, when you are the wounded one, it's hard to tell the difference. God commands us to be in community for this reason. He knows our emotions can deceive us.

Therefore, I need a healthy, godly circle of people around me. In these situations, I reach out to my mature Christian sisters and ask them what they see and hear coming from me. These insightful women love Jesus more than they love me. They can tell whether I have sincerely forgiven, or I'm just "white knuckling" it. They are usually the voice of truth in my ear.

Do you have that person in your life? If not, why not?

Sometimes, my husband can be a sounding board. However, if the situation includes his kids, he's frequently too emotionally attached to the circumstances to be objective.

As a young Christian, I was introduced to a woman who significantly impacted my life and journey with Jesus. I look forward to meeting her in heaven. Her name is Corrie Ten Boom, and she served time in a German concentration camp during World War II for the crime of hiding Jews in her home. After her release from prison, due to a clerical error, she traveled the world telling anyone who would listen, "there is no pit so deep that God is not deeper still."

I decided if this woman could hold onto her faith in Jesus after the torture, humiliation, and devastation she suffered, I wanted to learn more.

One of her greatest impacts on my life is her description of forgiveness. After one of her speaking events, God would test her willingness to live out what she was teaching and preaching. This is her story.

> "It was in a church in Munich that I saw him – a balding, heavyset man in a gray overcoat, brown felt hat clutched between his hands. People were filing out of the basement room where I had just spoken, moving along the rows of wooden chairs to the door at the rear. It was 1947 and I had come from Holland to defeated Germany with the message that God forgives.
>
> It was the truth. They needed most to hear in that bitter, bombed out land, and I gave them my favorite mental picture. Maybe because the sea is never far from a Hollanders, I like to think that that's where forgiven sins were thrown. When we confess our sins, I said, God cast them into the deepest ocean gone forever. And even though I cannot find a scripture for it, I believe God, then places assigned there that says, no fishing allowed. The solemn faces stared back at me, not quite daring to believe.
>
> There were never questions after a talk in Germany in 1947. People stood up in silence, and in silence collected their wraps, and in silence left the room. And that's when I saw him, working his way forward against the others. One moment I saw the overcoat and the brown hat: the next, a blue uniform, and a visor cap with its skull and crossbones. It came back with a rush, the huge room with its harsh overhead lights; the pathetic pile of dresses, and shoes at the center of the floor; the shame of walking naked past this man. I could see my sister's frail form ahead of me, sharp beneath the parchment skin. Betsy, how thin you were. The place was Ravensbruck and the man who was making his

way forward had been a guard – one of the cruelest guards. Now he was in front of me hand thrust out. *"Fine message Fraulein how good is it to know that, as you say, all our sins are at the bottom of the sea!"* And I, who had spoken so glibly of forgiveness, fumbled in my pocketbook rather than take that hand. He would not remember me, of course.

How could he remember one prisoner among those thousands of women?

But I remembered him and the leather crop swinging from his belt. I was face-to-face with one of my captors and my blood seemed to freeze.

"You mentioned Ravensbruck in your talk," he was saying *"I was a guard there."* No, he did not remember me.

"But since that time," he went on, *"I have become a Christian. I know that God has forgiven me for the cruel things I did there, but I would like to hear it from your lips as well. Fraulein"* and again the hand came out—*"will you forgive me?"*

And I stood there. I whose sins had again and again to be forgiven—and I could not forgive. Betsy had died in that place. Could he erase her slow, terrible death simply for the asking? It could not have been many seconds that he stood there, hand held out, but to me it seemed hours as I wrestled with the most difficult thing I had ever had to do.

For I had to do it - I knew that. The message that God forgives has a prior condition that we forgive those who have injured us. If you do not forgive men, their trespasses, Jesus says neither will your father and heaven forgive your trespasses. I knew it not only as a commandment of God, but as a daily experience. Since the end of the war, I had come home in Holland for victims of Nazi brutality. Those who were able to forgive their former enemies, were able to also return to the outside world and rebuild their lives, no *matter what the physical scars. Those who nursed their bitterness remained invalids. It was as simple and as horrible as that.*

And still, I stood there with the coldness clutching my heart. But forgiveness is not an emotion. I knew that too. Forgiveness is an act of the will, and the will can function, regardless of the temperature of the heart.

"Jesus, help me!" I prayed silently. I can lift my hand. I can do that much. You supply the feeling.

And so woodenly, mechanically, I thrust my hand into the one stretched out to me. And as I did an incredible thing took place. The current started in my shoulder, raced down my arm, sprang into our joined hands. And then this healing warmth seem to flood my whole being, bringing tears to my eyes. "I forgive you, brother!" I cried. "With all my heart."

For a long moment, we grasped each other's hands, the former guard, and the former prisoner. I had never known Gods love so intensely as I did them. But even so, I realized it was not my love. I had tried and did not have the power. It was the power of the Holy Spirit as recorded in Romans, 5:5 "because the love of God is she abroad in our hearts by the Holy Ghost, which is given to unto us."[8]

Did you need tissues while reading this? I do. Every. Single. Time.

If you love Jesus, you will recognize the power of His resurrection in this story. We do not forgive because of our own strength, ability, or desire. It is a surrendering. And it isn't conditional on how we feel or what the other person does afterwards.

---

8 Christian Literature Crusade and Fleming Revell Co., 1974, Tramp for the Lord, Corrie ten Boom, p 55-57

It's hard. Which is why we need God.

I often must pray, "Lord, make me willing to become willing to forgive this person." He has never failed.

WHAT DO WE LEARN FROM THIS STEPFAMILY?

- It's normal for families to hurt each other. We know each other intimately, and that makes us vulnerable.
- Sibling rivalry can run deep
- A parent's favoritism toward one child can create deep resentment
- A parent who speaks negative, condescending, humiliating words over their child can implant a self-loathing and shame that can last a lifetime.
- Setting healthy boundaries isn't sin.
- Blood connections run deep and aren't to be shamed or dismissed.
- God can teach me how to see the one who hurt me through his eyes, not mine.
- It's good for men to cry and grieve.
- Forgiveness sets me free and sometimes overcomes the wounds of the past.
- Forgiveness can bring goodness into the future

HOW DOES LEARNING ABOUT *THIS* STEPFAMILY STRENGTHEN *MY* STEPFAMILY?

- Learning how to forgive is a process. Have I asked God to forgive me?
- Do I have a distorted view of what it means to forgive?

- Is there someone in my stepfamily I need to forgive? What are the first steps I need to take?
- Do I need a good friend to come alongside me?
- Is the person who wounded me repentant? How does that affect my response?
- Why am I finding it so difficult to forgive this person? Do I have the false belief that I need to trust him/her again merely because I forgive?
- Are there things in my past that make it harder for me to trust myself with forgiveness? What am I doing to overcome those issues?
- What would it look like to have healthy, godly boundaries? Do I know how to set them? If not, how will I learn that? What if my spouse disagrees with my boundary and accuses me of being cruel?
- What is my response if my spouse refuses to acknowledge that his/her family is hurting me? How will I forgive my spouse for not standing beside me and supporting me?
- How can I tell if I've forgiven? What are the signs that I've stopped seeking revenge?

PRAYER

Lord, it's too big. Seriously. You don't really expect me to forgive in this situation, do you? I don't even know where to begin. And I don't want to forgive them. They don't deserve it. They aren't sorry.

And yet... You forgave and continue to forgive me when I don't deserve it.

Make me willing, Lord. Right now, I'm not even willing. But I know if I sincerely ask and humble myself, you will help me. You will do it through me.

I'm afraid, God. I'm terrified of getting hurt—again.

And yet, I'm asking. Make me willing, to become willing to forgive my spouse, my stepkids, the ex, the extended family, my biological family, anyone who is hurting me right now. Help me to see that person as you see them.

Open the eyes of my heart to see them with your unconditional love. And rather than worrying about protecting myself, let me see the bigger picture. Allow me to visualize the chains of unforgiveness around my ankles, wrists, and neck. And how they are keeping me a prisoner to this situation. Let me see into the heavenly realm where the battle between good and evil is taking place. Help me to recognize this person(s) is not my enemy. He/she is a wounded person lashing out, and I'm an easy target. Help me to set a godly boundary when one is needed and to walk away if that is necessary. I trust you, Lord. Help me. Amen.

~ 6 ~

OVERCOMING SHAME

King David Part 1 – Wives, Wives, and More Wives

In 2013, I had the glorious experience of visiting the Holy Land in Israel. One of my most profound memories was experiencing the tomb of King David in Mount Zion. I was shocked to observe numerous women rocking back and forth in front of his tomb. They were adorned with head coverings and chanting whispered prayers.

I had no idea there were people who still worshipped King David.

The Old Testament reveals that David was buried elsewhere. This site is directly underneath Cenacle, where Christians commemorate the Last Supper with Jesus. It is still a place of honor and pilgrimage for Jews, Muslims, and Christians.

I love King David. I relate to King David.

My heart is passionate for God, like his. No words describe how grateful I am for God's healing, forgiveness, and unconditional love over my life. He rescued me from a pit of despair that was so deep and dark it's hard to explain. And yet, in my human frailty, my mind can wander and lead me towards things that are not of him. My emotions, insecurities, and/or sin can take me down a destructive and dangerous road.

King David is my brother. His passion and audacious, extravagant adoration of God motivates me. I love how he runs after holiness with a fevered fixation. He's like a living, breathing burst of flamboyant God-formed firecrackers.

And then there are his flaws. I respond to his inadequacies. They should serve us as a warning. David reminds me that even the strongest, most passionate God-lover can make sinful choices if complacent or smug.

Even though David's life is filled with extraordinary, powerful victories, his sinful choices initiated monumental, long-term, disastrous consequences. His horrific actions created significant pain for himself and everyone around him. He's a perfect picture of what happens when we start doing things "my way" instead of God's. Our society teaches "what I do is none of your business." We ignore the truth that unless I live in a cave alone, my actions affect others. David is a blinking billboard, a lifesaving reminder to keep our relationship with God fresh and new daily. We cannot coast on yesterday's commitment. Unshakable faith comes from consistently spending time with Him. Even the ability to trust, follow, and love God comes from God. Developing a keen ear for his voice and crawling tightly into His arms are what keep us safe, alert, and alive.

David reveals how easy it is to casually slide into complacency and self-satisfaction. When we take our eyes off Jesus and look for satisfaction elsewhere, we are treading into dangerous territory.

David's life and stepfamily remind us why selfishness never ends well.

As a former legalistic Pharisee myself (I needed a 12-step program to overcome it), I want to be clear. God isn't seeking mindless, robotic soldiers who perform to perfection. He does desire that we remain close to Him and obey Him—for our own protection.

In the same way a parent warns a child obliviously running toward a toy in the middle of a busy street, God wants us to steer clear of the danger He sees that we don't.

God reveals the good and bad about David. The mighty man of God, in the genealogy of Jesus, is exposed.

We begin in 1 Samuel. The prophet Samuel is on a mission from God to replace King Saul. Samuel isn't excited about this task. If he's caught by the king, it means execution. But God tells him to go. He obeys.

We don't know David's mother, but many scholars believe she was previously married before the union to David's father Jesse. David had seven older brothers and two sisters. Some of these may have been half brothers and sisters, which would explain why he is the youngest.

Many accounts report that his sister Abigail and David had the same mother and a different father. Abigail's father is named Zeruiah Nahash. This means David had half-siblings. We don't know a lot about how they interacted as kids. However, we see conflict between them as adults. David is the youngest. He is likely viewed as an ours baby with Jesse. Therefore, David grew up in a stepfamily.

When Samuel arrives at Jesse's home, he is greatly honored. Jesse knows one of his own sons will be the king. He presents each of his sons before the prophet, starting with the oldest, as would be the custom.

God reveals as each son stands before Samuel, "Nope, that's not the one I've chosen. Keep going." Samuel passes over all the older brothers and asks Jesse if he has another son. Jesse is shocked. The only one left is David. The youngest, a little shepherd boy.

> *"So he sent for him and had him brought in. He was glowing with health and had a fine appearance and handsome features. Then the* Lord *said, "Rise and anoint him; this is the one." So Samuel took the horn of oil and anointed him in the presence of his brothers, and from that day on the Spirit of the* Lord *came powerfully upon David. Samuel then went to Ramah.* 1 Samuel 16:12-13

God chooses David to be the one. He will forever be listed as a "man after God's own heart."

Everyone, including dad, assumed one of the older brothers would be the chosen king.

God had other plans. He usually does.

God does not look through the same lens as man. We look at accomplishments, strength, charisma, appearance, money, influence, everything on the outside. God sees into a person's heart.

God created David in his mother's womb for such a time and place as this. And He knows the essence of the boy. God sees his core, his marrow, his soul.

Over David's lifetime, he endures many trials. When King Saul fears David will overthrow him as king, he attempts to kill him. David diligently and honorably remains faithful to King Saul, even when he doesn't deserve it.

We don't always know why God allows wicked men to rule. We are to remain like Christ regardless of who is on a human throne. Speaking truth or standing for righteousness doesn't mean behaving in a manner that is disrespectful, obnoxious, or vengeful.

And David honors God by honoring King Saul. David explicitly trusts God and embraces His sovereignty. Saul's reign and power are dictated by God. The monarchy is entirely in His hands. David's current job is to obey. Nothing more.

After many years, David comes into power as the king. He has many children with various women. Some are named, and many are not.

> *"After he left Hebron, David took more concubines and wives in Jerusalem, and more sons and daughters were born to him."* 2 Samuel 5:13

We won't explore every wife in David's stepfamily journey; some aren't mentioned in Scripture. However, it's important to understand the role each woman played in his life. David's stepfamilies reveal and teach a great deal about stepfamily living.

Michal

Michal is David's first wife. She is the daughter of King Saul, and she passionately loves David. However, her father's reasons for giving his daughter to David were an act of manipulation and control. His fear of young David's popularity prompted the union. She was used as a vehicle to get behind the door of David's life. The marriage was implemented as a strategic channel to inflict revenge on his rival and assassinate his new son-in-law. Saul hated David. He assumes his daughter will conform to his plot to kill him. However, his daughter was in love with her husband, and she had the courage to protect him.

"Now Saul's daughter Michal was in love with David." 1 Samuel 18:20

Interestingly, she is the only woman in the Bible described as having loved a man. We never read that David loved her back. We do know that this prize and being married to the King's daughter is a high honor. Shortly after the wedding, Michal overhears a plot, instigated by her father, to kill David. She helps him escape out a window, believing David will send for her eventually, and they will reunite. He did not. David doesn't look back. He goes into hiding and moves forward with his life. He leaves her behind. He marries other women, and they give him many children.

We don't hear about Michal again for a long time. David is gone and presumably out of her life. Her father, still the king, gives her in marriage to another man, Paltiel. She is the only woman in the Bible for whom the word polyandry (one woman married to several men at the same time) applies.

Eventually, King Saul dies, and the word of his death is delivered to David. He has finally defeated Saul and Saul's army. His enemies desire to make peace with David, and he agrees—on one condition. Saul's men need to give Michal back to David.

In David's mind, he had paid for her, and therefore, he still owns her. He probably wanted the king's daughter back as security and assurance to inherit the throne. He and Michel had never divorced. She was his insurance policy for the crown.

She is forcibly removed from her second husband, a man who sincerely loves her, and taken to King David. And poor, pitiful Paltiel is devastated.

The next scene between Michal and David reveals the tension between them. She mocks him with insults dripping in sarcasm. David is furious and retaliates.

The reunification with David, her first husband, obviously doesn't go well for Michal. Perhaps she blames him for taking her away from the man who truly loved her; perhaps she's still angry with his rejection of her. Maybe she's just miserable. We don't know for sure. We do know she never had any children, and on that day, it was a good reason to be irritable and despondent.

Even though Michal was the daughter and the wife of a king, the remainder of her life is described in one gloomy verse.

> *"And Michal daughter of Saul had no children to the day of her death."* 2 Samuel 6:23

Abigail

We meet one of David's wives, Abigail, in 1 Samuel. She originally was the wife of Nabal, a malicious man who disrespected David. In retaliation for his foolishness, David prepares to destroy his entire household. Then Nabal's beautiful, wise, and gracious wife Abigail appears. She humbly bows down all the way to the ground before David. She begs him not to seek revenge against her reckless husband. David recognizes her good judgment and relents. When Abigail explains to her hung-over husband how close he came to being annihilated, it sends Nabal into heart failure. Ten days later, he died.

After Nabal's death, David sends for her, and Abigail becomes one of his wives. God uses Abigail to help David, and he thanks her for her prudence, insight, and actions. He praises her. After Nabal's death, it's possible she would have inherited her husband's massive fortune, but that does not seem to matter. Scripture tells us that she immediately packs her bags, takes a few of her servants, and promptly goes with David's men, leaving everything behind. Later, she gives David a son.

Abigail's actions provide us with wisdom in various ways. The Bible describes Nabal as "a surly and mean man." We see in his response to David that he is arrogant and insulting.

Abigail must have experienced many emotions when she received news of the massive mess her husband had created. At the very least, she was embarrassed, ashamed, and nervous. Her quick response to fix the problem reveals she understood the danger her husband had created.

This was not the first time her husband had been mean and hurtful. Scripture tells us that even the servants understood his tyrannical conduct. He had an alarming temper and enjoyed inflicting terror. He abused his power, and his wife knew it well. She also recognized that it is unwise to address him in his altered state. Don't tackle the problem when the person is in an altered state. It's fruitless.

She wisely waits for the next morning.

When a spouse lives with an angry, demanding, controlling, vengeful partner, he/she learns to walk on eggshells as do the kids. In this home, only the abuser matters. The rest of the family lives in terror of the next outburst. And they become convinced that it will never end. Everyone walks on eggshells, afraid to "poke the bear." And it's all too common.

"My husband could care less how I feel," Emily shared. "If I attempt to share, he blames me for his actions. He retaliates by accusing me of being bipolar and tells me I need medication and therapy. Then he condemns me for having "mommy issues" that are a result of a horribly abusive childhood. That's his go-to comment after he's done ranting. He accuses me of being an immature baby with little girl problems, stating none of this has anything to do with him. I'm so confused. Maybe it is all my fault? But why does that nullify his behavior? If I do have mental issues, shouldn't he be kinder to me rather than meaner? He controls all our finances, so even if I wanted to get help, I couldn't. I have no resources. I'm trapped."

This is not marriage. God never designed marriage to be a prison sentence. Marriage is not one person dominating, controlling, and manipulating the other. That isn't love. It is hate.

Unfortunately, I understand this twisted perversion of love. I used to have the unquenchable need to rescue others, even when letting them experience the consequences of their own poor choices would have been wiser. It's a vicious cycle requiring God's revelation and rescue to overcome.

"My husband couldn't care less how I feel." Emily shared. "If I attempt to share my feelings, he blames me for his actions. Responds by saying I'm bipolar and that I need therapy. He blames his behavior on the fact that I had a horrible childhood and was abused. That's his go-to comment. That I'm an immature baby with little girl problems that have nothing to do with him. He controls all the money, so I couldn't even if I wanted to get help. I have no resources. I'm trapped."

This is not marriage. God never designed marriage to be a prison sentence. Marriage is not one person dominating, controlling, and manipulating the other. That isn't love. It is hate.

God uses Abigail to help David, and he thanks her for her prudence, insight, and actions. He praises her. And when he hears that her ruthless husband has died, he sends for Abigail to become his wife. She doesn't hesitate. It's possible she would have inherited her husband's massive fortune, but that does not seem to matter. Scripture tells us that she immediately packs her bags, takes a few of her servants, and promptly goes with David's men, leaving everything behind. Later, she gives David a son.

Bathsheba

The sad story of David's wife, Bathsheba, is well-known.

She was originally the wife of Uriah the Hittite, a trusted soldier in David's army.

In 2 Samuel 11, we read of David's poorest choices and sins.

He sees a woman bathing, and he wants her. Uriah was away at war. David knows she is another man's wife; however, in that moment of excitement, he doesn't care about anyone but himself. David summoned her to his palace and had intercourse with her. We must remember that women had no power. Women were property. There was no ability for her to say, "No, I'm not in the mood," especially to the king. This wasn't a decision Bathsheba made; she was beckoned and commanded.

Some theologians and teachers try to blame her equally. After a deep dive into the role and view of women in that day, I disagree. She had no choice.

It goes from bad to worse. Sin always does.

She gets pregnant and informs David. Rather than repent, he added more sins to this sin. David orders that Uriah be placed on the front lines of the battlefield and to be abandoned by his fellow soldiers and killed by the enemy. David murders him via war.

As we read this account of Bathsheba, it's important to note David's immorality started in his mind, not in his pants. Every sin ever committed begins in the same place. No one is different or escapes this truth.

If we learn to take those destructive thoughts captive immediately, we can escape many sorrows and hurtful choices.

However, there are times when we are more vulnerable to sin. We see it today when we read about pastor after pastor committing sins.

What caused David's tender soul to reach such an egotistical place of disobedience? Most theologians agree that David was compromised and at risk because of the following:

Isolation

Dave Edwards once said, "All rebellion begins in isolation." Dear brother and sister in Christ, if you hear nothing else from this study, please hear this warning. We, the Body of Jesus Christ, desperately need a live, authentic community. We must stop isolating; it is killing us. The enemy of our soul knows that isolation is his best breeding ground. It is where he obtains great victory. If he can get God's people to sequester, we are much more likely to listen to his lies. We become so lonely and trapped in despair, solitude, and fear that we seek relief from the pain in any way possible. Pain pursues pleasure. Anything that numbs the loneliness for a second, then two seconds, and then a lifetime becomes our master. Whether that be food, drugs, TV, exercise, pets, or the Internet. Satan doesn't care. If you are trapped into believing it is your SOURCE of companionship and relief rather than God, he's won.

David should have been with his men. He shouldn't have been without accountability. He saw how his mentor, Saul, crumbled under the weight of pride and overconfidence. It should have taught him to remain humble and accountable at all costs. He didn't.

Ignoring the Nudge

David had numerous opportunities to turn around. He could have confessed his immorality and made it right. He didn't. When we refuse to allow the Holy Spirit to convict us, His influence or nudge to our heart and mind becomes dull and easier to ignore. We eventually become numb to his holy pokes and prods. The longer we remain in disobedience, the greater danger we encounter. We can stifle and ignore God's conviction for long enough that the shame or healthy guilt that would usually bring us to our senses goes mute. It is at this point when we are in massive danger.

Wearing a Mask

When the Christ follower decides to follow society's view of right and wrong, rather than God's holy teachings, it requires a mask. The charade has begun, and the lies that lurk beneath are cloaked with a fake smile. We cover our shame and try to hide from God, just like Adam and Eve in the garden. Any conviction that might attempt to jar the mind back to truth and uproot the lie is obscured with justification, convenience, entitlement, and excuses. Hence the mask. Eventually, it gets hot and sweaty under the disguise, and living the lies becomes complex. However, the deception becomes routine. We have forgotten the free life, which was liberated from shame. The jailer has deceptively convinced us this is an abundant life. It's a trap. A fly in the spider's web. And the devil dances. He knows it's the pathway and vehicle to destruction.

This was the inception of David's problems.

This one foolish, all-consuming desire to have what God said he should not took him to places of unhappiness and sorrow he couldn't have dreamed. It was a crossroad moment in his life. And the consequences would haunt him until he died.

He believed he knew more than God. Again, we are back in the Garden thinking like Adam and Eve.

And that sin, and the pain it created, passed on for many generations.

Walking away from God's truth looks harmless. It's filled with promises of delight and pleasure. It woos with gratification all the while hiding the dagger that stabs precisely and unshakably through the heart and soul.

God is always willing to forgive us. But He doesn't eliminate the consequences.

David's power to have anything he wanted had consumed his mind. He believes he can do anything he pleases. Pride, self-absorption, and an inflated ego have taken down many a man or woman. And it's no different with our precious King David.

David orders the murder of Bathsheba's husband, Uriah. She is mourning his death. And then he marries her.

When Uriah's wife heard that her husband was dead, she mourned for him. After the time of mourning was over, David had her brought to his house, and she became his wife and bore him a son. But the thing David had done displeased the Lord. 2 Samuel 11:26-27.

God is upset with David, his chosen one. This should dispel any crazy notion our society teaches about God always being happy and pleased with us. When we sin, it breaks His heart. It grieves Him deeply.

Why? Because He's judgmental? Moody? A crybaby? A narcissist? No, because he is a good, holy, perfect Daddy. And He knows when we walk away from his instructions, we are headed for pain, sorrow, and trouble.

David marries Bathsheba, and she gives birth to the son conceived during his adultery. David assumes he has gotten away with the entire mess. His pride and cockiness grow.

But we must not miss what is taking place in him, internally. His soul is beginning to disturb him.

It is believed that he wrote Psalm 32:3-4 during this season of rebellion and unrepentance. It displays a man who is emotionally and physically sick.

Blessed is the one whose transgressions are forgiven, whose sins are covered.
Blessed is the one whose sin the Lord does not count against them and in whose spirit is no deceit.
When I kept silent, my bones wasted away through my groaning all day long
For day and night your hand was heavy on me; my strength was sapped as in the heat of summer
Then I acknowledged my sin to you and did not cover up my iniquity. I said, "I will confess my transgressions to the Lord."
And you forgave the guilt of my sin.
Therefore, let all the faithful pray to you while you may be found; surely the rising of the mighty waters will not reach them. Psalm 32:1-6

David understands. His words in this psalm are profound. And they go for the jugular vein into the heart of the matter.

Running from God can be haunting, exhausting, and debilitating. Sometimes, physical illness can manifest from our sins.

On the outside, David's pride, narcissism, and arrogance don't seem to affect him. On the inside, he is descending into an abyss.

This is when God calls Nathan, a godly man and prophet, to step up and confront David.

David is familiar with him. He trusts and respects the man. And God does what only He can do. He creates a scenario that requires David to point the accusing finger at himself. Nathan disguises a story so that David doesn't immediately recognize the mirror that is paralleling his own life.

Self-centeredness shrouds his mind with darkness. Arrogance veils God's anointed light. He can no longer think honorably, prudently, and divinely as he once did. Pride has robbed his judgment, humility, and astuteness.

After hearing Nathan's story, David proclaims a severe judgment over the culprit. Only to discover it is he, himself, who is the perpetrator.

A Moment of Reckoning

We must remember that God never stops loving David or Bathsheba during his rebellion. They are his children, and He has deep compassion for them. However, they are breaking His heart. David has purposefully wandered into the danger zone, and God knows it's time to wake him up.

If you are a parent, or you love a child as if they were your own, you understand. God loves this child more than you do. And He knows how and when to wake him/her up.

"Sometimes the further we wander outside God's will, the more we judge others and the less we show mercy. David was ready to find this man and kill him until he found out he was the man. What was God trying to accomplish? God wanted David to recognize that he deserved to die. Bathsheba deserved death according to Hebrew law. So did Joab for setting up another person's death. God allowed David to sit as judge over his own life and pronounce a death sentence on himself so his Heavenly Father could grant him the undeserved gift of life." [9]

---

9 Lifeway Press Resources, David, Seeking a Heart Like His, Beth Moore, 2010, p 159

David is now fully awake. The shock and reality of what he has done brings him to his knees. And the son he created with Bathsheba becomes extremely ill.

David's repentance to God is chronicled in Psalm 51.

For generations, his prayer has served God's people as a benchmark for awareness regarding the difference between merely saying "I'm sorry" and genuinely being remorseful. One comes as words from the mouth, the other is a lament from the heart. It's the distinction between sadness over getting caught, verses humbly crumbling to the floor in recognition of the offense.

When attempting to discern whether a person is truly repentant or merely trying to get past the offense, Psalm 51 serves as an excellent tool.

David takes full responsibility for his actions. He blames no one else.

Can Good Come from Evil?

In God's hands, the answer is yes. David and Bathsheba had four more children. And their son, Solomon, became a mighty king after his father's death. It is through this son we find the lineage of the Messiah, Jesus Christ.

Read that again.

One of the sons that came from David's marriage to Bathsheba is the lineage to Jesus Christ, the Savior of the world.

God uses everything. Although we do not escape the consequences of our sins, God can still use us for His good---If we repent, admit what we have done, and turn around.

This is very good news.

David is a different man after his son dies. He's not haughty or condescending. A season of disobedience can heal us from a judgmental or critical attitude. It reveals how anyone, even the godliest person, can be lured into sin.

Season of Rebellion

I've experienced a season of rebellion against God. Have you? It's horrible.

There is no one more miserable than a Christ follower who has chosen to turn away from God and live in disobedience.

My season still causes me to cry.

If, six months prior, someone had told me that I would soon fall into a state of debauchery, I would have laughed and said—never! I love Jesus too much. Never.

I was a baby Christian and a fool.

I didn't know that one day my first husband would announce an extramarital affair and leave me for another woman. I didn't know how those words and actions would demolish and annihilate my self-worth. In that shattered condition, I succumbed to disobedience in ways I never dreamed possible. When I read the words that I wrote in my journal during that dreadful time, I still cringe and weep. The shame is repulsive and overwhelming.

I'm grateful for God's forgiveness, redemption, and restoration. That unpleasant experience serves me well as a reminder to stay humble. When I'm tempted to believe I'm better than another, or a critical attitude is creeping in, I remember my poor choices. It's a holy slap to the soul.

In 2002, there was a story in the news about a woman named Clara Harris who saw her husband coming out of a hotel with his mistress. She knew he was having an affair. Seeing them together triggered her rage to a catastrophic level. She intentionally drove her car into her husband.

> *The first impact sent David Harris flying 25 feet. Then, prosecutors said Clara Harris crossed two grassy medians and ran over her husband three more times before she put*

the car in reverse and backed over his body, leaving the car parked on top of him.[10]

I remember reading this and saying out loud, "There but by the grace of God, go I."

I understand this woman's rage. I know what it felt like to be so out of control that you could do something desperately irrational. I am not advocating or justifying her actions. God would never condone her behavior.

But now I understand how easily, in one minute, life can change so drastically. And the shock renders us emotionally, mentally, and physically vulnerable.

I understand her brain in a way I never would have before my divorce.

Many stepfamilies understand this type of sudden amazement. Unlike a first marriage, we are consistently dealing with things from the other home that threaten to derail us. Sometimes, they infuriate us to the point of having drastic and damaging thoughts.

In God's hands, we cry out for the mind of Christ. God can teach us how to overcome evil with good. It's a promise.

Do not be overcome by evil, but overcome evil with good. Romans 12:21

It is possible. God can use the sin done to us—and the sin done by us—for a higher purpose, if we surrender, confess, heal, and hand the broken pieces to Him.

David shows us what it looks like to be used by God before, during, and after we sin. God never gives up. He never leaves us where He finds us.

---

10 https://abc7chicago.com/clara-harris-texas-dentist-kills-husband-today-david-run-over/12797294/

WHAT DO WE LEARN FROM THIS STEPFAMILY?

- It's wise to pay attention to David's slow drift away from God. He started out strong but didn't diligently nurture his daily relationship. He gradually coasted away.
- EVERYONE is vulnerable at some point. No human is above being tempted or placed in a circumstance that will feel overwhelming. Even Jesus was tempted in the wilderness for forty days and nights, but He didn't sin. Temptation is normal; we must learn how to resist.
- Rules rather than a relationship with God can easily create a blind spot in our spiritual life. Part of David's problem was that he knew the right things to do, but he let go of his passion for doing them.
- Yesterday's holiness is not enough to carry us through tomorrow's temptations. It's daily.
- Humility is the key to success. Psalm 51 is the road map.
- God uses a mighty man of God to confront David. We all need someone like this in our life.
- God forgives, but there are often lingering consequences to our actions.
- David isn't always a great husband, and it makes him vulnerable.

HOW DOES LEARNING ABOUT *THIS* STEPFAMILY STRENGTHEN *MY* STEPFAMILY?

Here comes the hard part. It's time to pause, do a deep dive, and get honest with God. It's time to think about your former marriage/relationship, your remarriage, and your kids/stepkids.,

- The first step to moving forward is with clean hands and a clean heart. Read out loud Psalm 51. Ask God to help you to admit any unconfessed sin. That requires honesty, especially if it's painful.
- Are you a bully like Nabal? Are you an enabler like Abigail? How would your closest friends answer those questions about you? How is this affecting your stepfamily?
- What did the prayer stir in your heart? Are there people you need to speak to about forgiveness, repentance, and restoration? Have you apologized to your kids for your role in the other parent's divorce? Apologize. If you sinned during your first marriage, even if it wasn't the reason the marriage died, confess it. The tendency is to sweep it under the rug and blame the ex-spouse. If you want a healthy relationship with your kids, they need to see a parent who admits when he/she is wrong.
- Am I teachable? Am I eager to learn what I don't know, or do I insist that my way of thinking is the best? Do I resist information that implies I may need to change?
- Don't let fear or shame incapacitate you. Jesus died to set you free. Don't let Satan shackle you. Tell your kids what you wish YOU had done differently and what you have learned since the divorce. Ask your child, "What do you wish I had done differently during the divorce with your mom/dad?"
- Score your marriage. Ask your spouse on a scale of 1-10 how healthy he/she thinks the marriage is. How does your score compare to your spouse's score? If there is a big difference, are you willing to discover why?

- When we have unresolved, embedded issues, they travel into the next marriage. When we ignore, deny, or forbid those issues to be healed, they spew out into our marriage and kids. What hidden emotions are affecting your marriage, spouse, and kids/stepkids?
- Does your spouse attempt to tell you areas of concern, but you refuse to discuss them? Why do you believe ignoring them is healthy, godly, or wise?
- Move forward. Ask God what it means and how to let go of your past. When we say we can't be forgiven, we are saying that the price Jesus paid for us wasn't enough. In essence, we are saying, "My sin is so horrible that His shed blood isn't enough to heal it." Do you really want to believe that? No? Then stop accepting the lie.

PRAYER

God, this is a wake-up call for me. I don't like it.

I realize I need to be aware of how my thinking and choices affect not only me but those around me. I don't like this feeling. It's dirty, ugly, and filled with shame. I want to crawl under the covers and never come out.

But today, I will choose differently.

I will believe what you say about my sin. I trust you, Jesus. And right this minute I confess my sins to you. I was wrong. I am to blame, no one else. I lay my disobedience down at the foot of your cross. I pray for the blood of Jesus Christ to pour over my sins and completely cleanse me. I thank you that nothing I've done is more significant, or more powerful, than the price you paid to cleanse me from that sin.

I'm done blaming others, including my ex-spouse. I'm finished focusing on what others are, or are not, doing.

That isn't my job, it's yours. Today, I'm focusing on what you want ME to do. If I need to apologize, teach me how and give me the words or actions. If I need to make restitution another way, I'm listening to your guidance. If I need to confess and ask for forgiveness from my kids, stepkids, or any other family member, I will do it.

I want you, Jesus. Just you. I want to be cleansed from all sin so I can walk freely in the abundant life you promise.

Today, it begins with me. I surrender. Amen.

~ 7 ~
Overcoming Failure
King David Part 2 – Poor Choices

"I only see my two kids twelve days a month," the dad shared. "I want them to look forward to spending time together. Sure, I let them stay up late and eat pizza most nights. And I don't expect them to show me their phones or who they're texting. That's because I trust my kids.

"But my wife doesn't agree with any of this. She thinks I'm letting them get away with murder. I think she's too strict. It's causing huge fights between us," he continued.

"I want to respect her opinion, but not at the risk of losing my children. I'm afraid if she keeps nagging them to do chores and limits their access to the Internet, they will refuse to come to our home. The kids have already told their mom that they don't like coming to our house anymore because my wife is mean to them. I don't know what to do. I feel trapped between honoring my wife and loving my kids. Seriously, is pizza or a cell phone that important? Why can't my wife understand my position and have some compassion for my children? After all, she's the adult."

Co-parenting with another home and former partner is exceedingly difficult. It is one of the reasons why God hates divorce (He doesn't hate divorced people). It's hard on everyone, especially the children. A parent must be in an emotionally healthy, stable, calm place to set a great parenting plan in motion. If mom or dad is willing to co-parent and compromise with the other home, that's the best scenario for everyone.

When negative emotions overwhelm our parenting judgment, it's easy for a parenting paralysis to set in. Leniency and indulgence follow closely behind. Paralyzed parents are unable to wisely assess when it's best to set a boundary and when it's okay to let it go.

After a divorce, the most common reason why parents, especially dads, don't implement boundaries with their kids is a fear the child will stop spending time together. Or even worse, the child could choose to live with the other parent full-time.

This unstable parenting perspective creates a sense of apathy, lethargy, exhaustion, and defeat. The parent faces a delicate and fragile dance between being too harsh or too soft. And it's not uncommon for the stepparent to feel he or she is too permissive. This is especially true if the spouse has a different standard of discipline with the stepkids or an ours baby.

When a child lives in two homes, with two sets of rules and expectations, it's common for a parent to resist setting boundaries and say no to the child. They don't want the time together to be crammed with rules and regulations, strict chores, and strict guidelines. Translation: They want the kids to have fun, eat whatever they want, and avoid situations that inflict tension or conflict.

This is frequently referred to as a Paralyzed Parent or Guilty Parent Syndrome.

"Guilty Father Syndrome occurs when a divorced father's guilt about his family breaking apart manifests in his uncontrollable need to please the emotionally wounded children. Aware of the emotional toll of divorce, guilty fathers vie for favorite-parent status by indulging a child's every whim. He simultaneously becomes a toy store, ATM, and doormat. Guilty fathers toss discipline out the window, avoid enforcing household rules, and spoil their kids with heaps of material items. Even worse, they completely abdicate the heavy lifting of parenting, allowing the new wife to take on a dreaded new role: 'The Enforcer.'"[11]

When a parent refuses to parent, the stepparent typically labels the partner as pathetic, cowardly, infuriating, and weak. He or she perceives the stepchild as dictating and/or manipulating the entire home. This creates blame, resentment, and sometimes loathing towards the stepchild when the root of the problem is the spouse.

This is the number one stressor for stepfamilies.

And it continues far into the adult years. Even if the kids aren't in the home, adult kids can create as much or more chaos and stress for the blended couple than little ones.

David's adult kids reap the consequences of their dad's unwillingness to parent.

My friend and co-author, Ron L Deal, explains it beautifully:

> *A paralyzed parent enables misbehavior which will undoubtedly escalate and worsen over time. This is particularly difficult when a paralyzed single parent remarries. The new stepparent is set-up for defeat when they bring the child's outrageous behavior to the attention of the biological parent. They are often met with defensiveness ("he's not selfish,*

---

[11] https://www.huffpost.com/entry/guilty-father-syndrome_b_839751

he's just going through a rough time"), counter-blame ("you just don't like my son"), or passive-aggressive patronizing (agreeing to discipline and then not following through). Further, the child will likely exploit the divided parental team, disrespect the stepparent, and stiff-arm the stepparent keeping them emotionally distant. But perhaps the most ironic result of paralyzed parenting (that is justified by the belief that it somehow reduces the child's emotional pain) is that it unwittingly prolongs a child's hurt, anger, and sadness over the past because they are never purposed to manage it responsibly. A child whose "depression over the divorce" excuses irresponsibility without consequence is not motivated to act better. Likewise, a child who hits or openly mistreats his stepsiblings without consequence will continue to "be mad" about how "unfair" life has been to him or her. Children, rather, need parents who boldly respond with firm and loving consequence to the child's behavior, As I like to say, "Just because you get handed a guilt-trip ticket, doesn't mean you have to go for the ride."[12]

Psychology Today, lists the most common reasons for GPS:

- I wasn't there enough.
- I didn't listen.
- I was too focused on the house and work.
- I wasn't affectionate enough.
- I was critical.
- I yelled, hit, and blamed.
- I was a bad role model.

---

12 https://smartstepfamilies.com/smart-help/learn/parenting-stepparenting/paralyzed-parenting-stepfamilies-when-you-don-t-follow-through

- I didn't take the time to understand my children.
- I wasn't consistent
- I pushed too hard.
- I didn't push enough.
- I spanked.
- I drank.
- I was depressed.
- I fought with my children's dad or mom.
- I got divorced.
- I said hurtful things.
- I was selfish.
- I ignored my child.
- I didn't protect my children.[13]

When you add in the stepfamily dynamics, there are additional burdens such as:

- My new spouse doesn't love my child
- My spouse is to mean to my child
- I'm now divided between my spouse and my child
- I'm not co-parenting well
- The stepkids are exposing my child to ungodly things
- My child now has mental illnesses because of the blend
- My remarriage has robbed my child of a peaceful home
- My child now feels "less than" because of the stepfamily

In our current society, this syndrome has reached epidemic levels, and stepfamilies present the most cases.

---

[13] Psychology Today https://www.psychologytoday.com/us/blog/healthy-connections/201109/are-you-guilty-parent

However, God reveals through King David that this is not a new conundrum. It plagued him thousands of years ago.

Perhaps one of the most telling illustrations of David's weakness as a dad is the situation between his two children (half-siblings) Amnon and Tamar.

Amnon was David's firstborn by his wife Ahinoam. Amnon plots a trick on David and his half-sister, Tamar, by pretending to be sick. David asks his daughter to bring Amnon some food to help him recover. And while she is in the room alone with her half-brother, the unspeakable happens. He rapes her. She begs for him to stop, but he refuses.

> *"No, my brother!" she said to him. "Don't force me! Such a thing should not be done in Israel! Don't do this wicked thing. What about me? Where could I get rid of my disgrace? And what about you? You would be like one of the wicked fools in Israel. Please speak to the king; he will not keep me from being married to you." But he refused to listen to her, and since he was stronger than she, he raped her.*
>
> *Then Amnon hated her with intense hatred. In fact, he hated her more than he had loved her. Amnon said to her, "Get up and get out!"*
>
> *"No!" she said to him. "Sending me away would be a greater wrong than what you have already done to me." But he refused to listen to her. He called his personal servant and said, "Get this woman out of my sight and bolt the door after her." So his servant put her out and bolted the door after her. She was wearing an ornate robe, for this was the kind of garment the virgin daughters of the king wore.*
> 2 Samuel 13:14-18

Amnon is a despicable man who ignores his sister's begging him to stop. He knew this act of violence against

Tamar not only assaults her body, but it will also destroy her entire life. In that day, a virgin was the only woman qualified for marriage, even if she's the king's daughter. This savagery renders as damaged goods. He obliterates her ability to marry and have children. He doesn't care. He continues to rape his half-sister Tamar, the daughter of Maakah.

As if the violation isn't bad enough, he is unrepentant and hateful towards her afterwards. He could have married her, restoring her honor. She pleads with him to stop destroying her life and rendering her a reject.

He is cruel and merciless. He callously refuses.

Tamar's full brother, Absalom, finds out about the rape. Furious, he takes his wounded, abandoned sister into his home. Even though she is the king's daughter, she is alone with no one to provide for her. She will never have a husband, family, or legacy. Scripture describes her as a desolate woman.

To make matters worse, her own father, King David, the person with all the power, does nothing. He is enraged but does absolutely nothing.

> *When King David heard all this, he was furious. And Absalom never said a word to Amnon, either good or bad; he hated Amnon because he had disgraced his sister Tamar.*
> 2 Samuel 13:21-22.

King David heard it all. He could have forced Amnon to marry her. He could have implemented a consequence against his wicked son's immoral and deviant actions. As the King, he had utmost power.

But he doesn't.

He allows his son to go on with life as usual. And because he won't do what a father should do to protect his child, a hatred grows between the two half-brothers. Amnon and Absalom are bitter enemies.

It's a massive mistake, and it comes back to haunt David in catastrophic ways in the future.

Most of us are wondering, "Why didn't he do anything? Why doesn't he severely reprimand his son for violating his beautiful, virginal daughter?"

I don't know.

I do know that this is one of David's biggest failures as a father. Neglecting his responsibility as a father is a big mistake.

Unfortunately, I see it all too often in my work with stepfamilies. Dad is either afraid or unwilling to discipline his kids. This is called enabling.

When a parent refuses to implement a consequence for their child after he or she sins, it affects everyone in the family. And there are long-term consequences.

In a second marriage, or blended families, it's common for at least one biological parent to refrain from healthy parenting. Kids need loving boundaries and healthy consequences to become mature adults.

Absalom watched his father do nothing when his half-brother raped his sister. His bitterness and need for revenge took root and grew. Enraged, he watched his depressed sister, year after year, morph into a shell of her former self. His fury grows into a full fire of revenge. Tamar merely existed. She didn't live anymore. Her laughter and jovial personality are replaced with tears, isolation, and devastation.

The seething against his brother brewed and expanded into a scheme to take revenge. And when the moment was right, and Amnon was drunk and vulnerable, Absalom killed his half-brother. 2 Samuel 13

By the end of the story, Absalom's heart is so callous and cold-blooded he's portrayed as a man consumed with fury.

David thinks he has only lost his son, Amnon. However, his enabling and lack of implementing a consequence and justice for Tamar eventually cost him both sons—one to death, the other to rage and indifference.

Absalom's contempt and rage don't end there. He attempts to ambush and kill his father, King David. He fails and is murdered instead.

David doesn't rejoice when his life is spared. He is completely heartbroken. Another son is dead. His face is to the ground.

> *The king was shaken. He went up to the room over the gateway and wept. As he went, he said: "O my son Absalom! My son, my son Absalom! If only I had died instead of you—O Absalom, my son, my son!"* 2 Samuel 18:33

This is not a happy ending. I'm crying as I type the words. I can almost hear him shrieking in grief.

God intends it to be a teachable moment for us.

Learn from it. Avoid it. Run from it.

I know many adult kids of divorce who no longer have any relationship with one or both parents. Sometimes, it's because the other parent brainwashed the child to hate and alienate a parent. Sometimes, it's because the parent refused to learn how to become a good parent. Sometimes, it's because the parent was unteachable and wouldn't listen to their spouse, friend, pastor, or anyone else who tried to explain the error.

Oftentimes, it's because the adult child's heart is still wounded, and they haven't healed yet. They don't know how.

The purpose of studying David isn't to heap more shame and embarrassment on a parent or stepfamily. God never wants us to live in shame; that's Satan's plan. God wants us free from humiliation.

Liberation from past mistakes happens when we learn and choose to make better choices. God uses David's flaws and disasters to teach us.

Discover how to discern the difference between loving, grace-filled, stable parenting versus enabling, permissive, and lax parenting. For many parents, the launching pad for a healthy stepfamily is recognizing and admitting they are parenting from an unhealthy place of pain, guilt, and laziness.

For some, reading about David's life without becoming discouraged is hard. If your children are grown, or you don't have a relationship, it may bring discouragement.

I have discovered that kids, even adult kids, want to see and hear a parent apologize. They long for the parent to take ownership in the part he or she played in hurting them. You can't fix what you refuse to admit.

God loves you; He has a good plan for you and your children. Kids are frequently willing to forgive a parent once they see true repentance rather than making excuses or blaming another parent.

God can and will teach you how to be a healthy, stable, godly parent if you ask. It's never too late.

WHAT DO WE LEARN FROM THIS STEPFAMILY?

- David was a great king but a horrible father. It is very easy, especially for men, to place their value and worth in a job or career. This is what David did, and it destroyed his family.
- It's not uncommon for parents to THINK they know what their child needs, yet the child craves something else. David didn't know his kids.

- What would have gone differently if David had acknowledged his mistake and apologized to Absalom for not recusing Tamar? What actions could David have taken to display his willingness to make things right after admitting guilt? What could David have done for Tamar to reveal his sorrow for her? I highly recommend Dr. Michelle Watson Canfield, the Dad Whisperer, for dads who have daughters (any age). She provides fabulous insight on what girls and women need from a dad on her website, TheDadWhisperer.com.
- David swept the issues under the rug, and disaster resulted. Why is this a common practice?
- David loved his kids. But many of his choices don't reveal it.
- David had leadership skills on the battlefield but not at home.
- Paralyzed parenting is as old as King David. Analyze why it's so common.

HOW DOES LEARNING ABOUT *THIS* STEPFAMILY STRENGTHEN *MY* STEPFAMILY?

- Address the issues. If you quickly jumped into a new remarriage and the kids felt ambushed, don't wait any longer to address it. Ask how they feel about having a stepparent. Ask what would make the transition easier. Share what you've learned about stepfamilies and how you understand why it may have been a shock to them.
- Discover who your kids are and how they express grief. Kids have tremendous sorrow after their

family splits up. Parents often don't want to discuss it because it makes them sad to hear what the divorce has created in the child. Avoidance is a colossal mistake. Let your child know that you see their pain, hear their lament, and want to comfort them, but you won't be a pushover and let guilt keep you from raising them with respect.

- Often, we parent based on how we were raised. Have I discovered and healed from my own childhood pain so that I don't pass it on to my kids?
- Do I know what an enabling is and how it forms? Am I a people pleaser? Is my spouse telling me I'm too lenient with the kids?
- Listen to podcasts or read great books on setting boundaries with kids. It helps to have a plan and structure. The younger they are, the easier it will become.
- Although we don't directly address this subject in David's story, it addresses the difference between parenting and stepparenting. Parents see their kids through a very different lens than a stepparent's perspective. This can create hurt feelings. The parent's primary emotion when looking at their child is love. A stepparent's initial emotion is responsibility. The parent wants the child first and foremost to know they are loved. The stepparent prioritizes learning to respect others and learning responsibility. Both have value. Unfortunately, one is emotional, and the other is a task. This is why a parent can become too soft and lenient with parenting; he or she doesn't want to hurt the child. The opposite is true for the stepparent. He or she wants the child to grow up and become mature and a responsible human being. There is the rub. Rules without relationships cause

rebellion. If the stepparent hasn't taken the time to build a strong bond with the stepchild before attempting to set boundaries and discipline, it frequently backfires. This causes the stepparent to be viewed as a dictator or bully.

Even when a biological mom and dad disagree about parenting, you never hear one parent say to the other, "You don't love this child." Love is a given. But it's a common issue in blended families. Why? Because it's true. A stepparent often doesn't have the same connection (especially in the beginning) to a stepchild that a biological parent would. To insist that a man or woman instantly have the same connection and love for a child they didn't birth, or barely know, as they would their own DNA is unwise. Yet, society implies and demands that stepparents have these same emotions.

What's a Parent to Do?

Because guilty parenting is so prevalent in today's world, how does a parent overcome feelings of guilt associated with the kids? How does a single or remarried parent learn to set healthy, appropriate boundaries?

- Acknowledge: The first step is to admit what you are currently doing isn't working.
- Seek God's wisdom: There isn't one situation in life where God isn't eager and willing to help us. That includes teaching us where we have erroneous thinking and how to change the mindset.
- Learn about kids and divorce. Most parents don't want to discuss how divorce has affected their kids. It's a huge mistake. Learning what a child's brain

thinks and processes is key to discovering how a parent can assist the child. www.DC4K.org is an excellent resource.

- Attend classes: There are excellent resources designed to set boundaries with kids. These classes must be modified to adjust to the child living in two homes. And that makes it exceedingly more difficult but not impossible.
- Dig down: It's not uncommon for our childhood pain to influence our parenting and stepparenting. Ask God to help you discover if there are hidden wounds that are affecting your parenting style or decision making.
- Communicate with your spouse: Chances are very good that your spouse has a different parenting plan and structure for implementing his/her plan. There isn't one way to raise kids, and having differing views is great. If everyone is under one roof, there needs to be a general "boundary" for certain things
- Respect your spouse's needs: If your husband hates it when a kid leaves a bike in the driveway, it's good to respect his need. If your wife can't tolerate dirty dishes in the bedroom, it's wise to implement a 'no food outside the kitchen' policy. If you do not want to hold your kids responsible for those tasks, then you should do them as the parent.
- Listen to your spouse: A stepparent can often see things that a biological parent can't. Especially a parent who is struggling with guilt or shame. Even when it's hard to hear, listen. God will use your spouse to help raise your child. God can use your spouse to prevent calamity. Sometimes, a stepparent is too harsh or controlling. However, it doesn't mean everything they share is inaccurate.

- Determine the "hill to die on": It's easy to discuss a strategy and formulate a plan; it's much harder to execute. Communicating what you can and cannot tolerate and what for each spouse is a hill to die on is crucial. For example, I would not tolerate illegal drugs or kids having sex in my home. For me, it's a hill to die on. My spouse needs to agree, accept that boundary, and implement a consequence if his child crosses that line.
- Too many hills: The mistake many stepparents make is for everything to become "a hill to die on." Then the parent resents the overwhelming plethora of rules. Stepparents become annoyed by things that frequently don't bother the parent, such as table manners, cleanliness, clothing style, hair, and food choices.

Note to Stepparents

I wonder what Bathsheba thought when David's two sons were duking it out. Or what she pondered when his son, Absalom, was trying to kill her husband. I'm sure she was furious that her stepsons behaved this way.

I wouldn't be surprised if David came home, laid his head in her lap, and cried over his sons.

As the stepparent, my job is to lovingly support my spouse and commit to becoming the best parent God has designed for me.

However, what is a stepparent to do when the spouse doesn't agree with his/her boundaries? Stepparent, if what the child is doing isn't harming you, your children, your pets, or your personal items, you must step back. If the parent(s) do not view the situation as a problem, the stepparent needs to disengage from the situation. Drop it. Walk away. It is not your child. When the parent prefers to handle it in a way that doesn't align with your perspective, agree to disagree.

The parent is accountable to God, not you. If they are making a mistake, that is between them and God.

If it harms your children, counseling is likely needed to come to other solutions. It is your job to protect your kids.

PRAYER

Dear God, I must humbly come to you now and say how grateful I am for your forgiveness and new life in Christ. Like David, I can easily get caught up in arrogance and self-centeredness. Remind me that everything I have and am is because you love and reconcile me to yourself. I am a new creation because you allowed and ordained it for me. I have no ability on my own to fight the temptation to take things into my own hands.

Lord, when I desire to retaliate, remind me that you alone are the one who knows what to do. Vengeance is yours—not mine. My job is to stay hidden in Christ so that you can pull me back from the ledge when the enemy tempts me to strike back or indulge in the things I think will make me happy.

Lord, if I am an enabler, heal me. If I think it's my job to cover for and protect those I shouldn't, I need to understand. It's a hard pattern to break, but I'm willing. And you are able. Nothing is too hard for you.

Show me the areas where I have made choices that have harmed my family, and when possible, show me how to rectify them.

Let me lead by example. Let me shine Christ into my family with your perfect balance of grace and truth. Help me to release the need to be right.

God, please don't let me spiral into despair over what I've done wrong as a parent. Don't let it crush me. You can redeem anything. You take the broken pieces and make something beautiful. You are my hope.

Remind me that you see my family through a different and perfect lens. I see them through my hurtful experiences. I see them through how they have wounded me.

I want to be holy as you are holy. It is the desire of my heart.

Make me like you, Jesus. Amen.

~ 8 ~

OVERCOMING INSULTS

Jesus and His Half-Siblings

Can you imagine being the half-brother or half-sister to Jesus Christ?

I mean, seriously. Talk about pressure.

Were his siblings jealous of Him? Was Mary able to love all of them equally? Did she favor the flawless son? Was Joseph intimidated or insecure about parenting the Son of God? Was he envious of Mary's favor from God, or did he view it as a privilege to be married to her?

We don't know much about Jesus as a child; we only read about his childhood a few times.

The first is on a trip to a big city. Mary and Joseph realize he's missing from the caravan on the ride home. They go back frantically looking for him. (Think of it as losing your child at Grand Central Station in NYC) When they find him, Jesus is inside the temple, teaching.

At the age of twelve.

Can't you just hear his siblings on the ride home from church?

"Of course, He was in the temple teaching the rabbis. Where else would he be? Who does he think he is teaching the holy men?"

"He's just showing off—the perfect 'Mama's boy.'"

"Jesus thinks he's better than anyone else. He must be a brat when we aren't looking. Nobody is that good. All. The. Time.

If you have siblings, you know these comments are what most parents hear.

Some denominations teach that Jesus didn't have brothers and sisters. However, most theologians agree that there is plenty of evidence in the Bible that Mary and Joseph had more children after Jesus was born.

Jesus' half-siblings are mentioned as accompanying Jesus and his mother to Capernaum after the marriage at Cana. (John 2:12)

Later, Mary and these same half-brothers ask to speak with Jesus. (Matthew 12:46-50; Mark 3:31-35; Luke 8:19-21)

Then we see his half-siblings pressuring Jesus to prove His Messiahship, which they doubted. (John 7:3-5)

After His crucifixion and death, these family members did come to believe that He was the Messiah and Savior. We read the book of Acts of them uniting with the other disciples before Pentecost. (Acts 1:13-14)

And then a few years later, Paul mentions the half-brother of Jesus,

> *"Then after three years, I went up to Jerusalem to get acquainted with Cephas and stayed with him fifteen days. I saw none of the other apostles—only James, the Lord's brother."* Galatians 1:18-19

All four Gospel writers specifically mention Jesus as having biological brothers. In addition, the first-century Jewish Historian Josephus mentions James, the brother of Jesus, offering additional support for this historical fact.

In addition to four brothers specifically mentioned in the New Testament, Jesus is also noted as having more than one sister:

"And are not all his sisters with us?" (Matthew 13:56)

Though unnamed, the plural form of sisters indicates more than one.

If you do not believe Jesus had half-siblings, it is your prerogative.

His Parents

Can you imagine the first time Mary and Joseph told their kids who Jesus is?

"Ummm... boys and girls gather around. It's time for a family meeting. Let's see, where should I begin? Well, your mother and I didn't consummate our marriage until after Jesus was born," Joseph announced.

"And the reason is... wow, this sounds strange, doesn't it? OK, let me put it this way: your oldest brother, Jesus, He's... ahhh, you may have noticed He's a bit different from others. He's, you are going to think this is crazy but, He's... He's... the SON OF GOD."

"Whaaat?" the siblings roared with laughter while rolling around on the floor.

"Yes, I know it sounds unbelievable. But it's true. God chose your mother to birth the long-awaited Messiah," Joseph continued.

"You aren't serious about this, are you, Abba? You can't be serious. It's just Jesus—our brother. He's no God," brother James probed.

"But everyone around here treats Him like He's perfect." Matthew chided under his breath.

Maybe it didn't happen like that at all. Perhaps the kids grew up and were told from birth that Jesus was the One sent by God to save them from their sins. We aren't privy to those details.

What we do know is His brothers didn't treat Him well.

I imagine, as any family with a gifted child, the siblings didn't like it. They were likely envious, jealous, and resentful of Jesus. What we do know and read is their response. As adults, his half-siblings treated Jesus poorly.

In the Beginning

It's lonely at the top.

> *For even his own brothers did not believe in him.* John 7:1-5

And when Jesus needed his half-siblings the most, they weren't there for him.

> *After this, Jesus went around in Galilee. He did not want to go about in Judea because the Jewish leaders there were looking for a way to kill him. But when the Jewish Festival of Tabernacles was near, Jesus' brothers said to him, "Leave Galilee and go to Judea, so that your disciples there may see the works you do. No one who wants to become a public figure act in secret. Since you are doing these things, show yourself to the world." For even his own brothers did not believe in him.*

At first glance, this doesn't seem like a big deal. It is. The half-brothers to Jesus did not support him. Whether it was fear, lack of faith, or resentment, there was no warm fuzzy reaction from his kin. He didn't feel the love when it came to his own DNA.

Why?

Here are some things we learn from John 7:

- His brothers didn't protect Him.
- They knew the people, including the religious leaders, were looking to kill him. And yet they walked away.
- His brothers mocked Him.
- It's normal for brothers to taunt each other. This went further. They are mocking his claim that he's the Savior
- His brothers accused Him of pride and self-glorification.
- "Since you are doing these things, show yourself to the world" is an attempt at a veiled accusation. Like when a nasty woman from the south says in her catty drawl, "Bless your heart." It's an allegation, not an affirmation.
- His brothers didn't trust or believe in Him.

John 7:5 declares their heartfelt thoughts and emotions. It reveals their disdain in an undeniable way. His brothers did not fear God.

With Mary and Joseph as the parents of this group, I'm not sure why they didn't have more faith. But for some reason, it happened. This should encourage Christian parents who have a prodigal child.

Eventually, his blended family saw miracle after miracle, especially towards the end of his life. They witnessed things no man, not even the priests, could describe. They learned of the blind receiving their sight, people being healed, and individuals being brought back from the dead. Yet they chose to reject Jesus. Not only did they doubt Jesus' words, but they questioned Mary's truthfulness, too. She's the one telling them how He came into the world.

They questioned the character of Jesus and their parents. When our deepest motives are scrutinized and dissected, it's exceedingly painful, especially if you're innocent of the charges.

Personally, it drops me to my knees. My character is everything. You can disagree with my thoughts or beliefs, but when you accuse me of deceit and deception or attack my motives or integrity, I no longer trust you.

Have you ever had people in your own family ridicule you? It hurts. Badly. Your home is supposed to be the safe place to fall when the world is falling apart. It's supposed to be a haven of shelter where we are secure and shielded from the world's cruelty.

That's not how Jesus's stepfamily responded.

We don't see his half-siblings at the foot of the cross, even when their widowed mother must witness the Roman soldiers ravage and brutalize their brother's body. They are nowhere to be found. They don't observe the iron against iron as the nails pulverize and conquer their brother's wrists and ankles. They don't hear Jesus' scream in agony as searing pain shoots through his nerves.

Just like the disciples, they are absent.

To be fair, they were likely terrified of being associated with him. It is safe to assume they also feared the religious leaders who just sent Jesus to his execution. Being his blood brothers, even if they didn't follow him, placed a target on their backs. Guilt by association was a real problem.

As Jesus hangs on the cross, He hands the care and protection of his mother, Mary, over to John, the youngest disciple. This is the clearest revelation that Joseph, Jesus's stepfather, has died. Somewhere between Jesus was teaching in the temple at age 12, and now, Mary lost her beloved Joseph.

Women in that time, especially widows, were exceedingly vulnerable. They needed protection. They were viewed as possessions and assets. After a husband died, the job of her wellbeing went to the oldest son. Since Mary's other sons aren't present, Jesus handed her to a person He trusted.

But it should have been one of his half-brothers—a biological son to Mary.

He was a good Jewish boy.

How sad. Is it not enough he's being humiliated, whipped, hammered, and crucified? He's got to take care of His mama? Unthinkable. But true.

And although his half-siblings were not there for His horrific death, we do see them later.

After the Resurrection

The grace and forgiveness Jesus bestows on his half-brothers after He rises from the dead is profound and humbling. As the gospels continue, we read where at least some of His half-siblings recognize and proclaim who He is.

I can only imagine what it would have been like to realize your half-brother is the Messiah. And the crushing shame and fear which likely followed.

What might he do to us for not believing? Will He forgive us? Will He embrace us? Should I stand behind my mother for protection?

Jesus reveals who He is. And He is Good. Very good.

As always, Jesus is our example of how to respond when a loved one rejects us.

His family is safe because he is trustworthy. He is permanent. He is the Rock Eternal.

Even when insulted, rejected, dismissed, and disregarded, Jesus still loves them.

I don't know how, other than it's a God thing.

On human strength alone, it's impossible to do consistently.

If I'm a Christian and hungering to be like Jesus, He will teach me how to do it too.

"Laura, my husband's family is very rude to me. I know they adored his first wife," Michaela stated. "They either ignore me completely and pretend I don't exist, or they say vicious things to my face. I'm trying to respond as Jesus would, but I don't know if I can continue to be around them. My husband wants me to attend family functions with him, so I keep going. Now, a baby shower is coming up for one of his nieces, and I don't want to attend. I try to tell him how much their rejection hurts me, but he becomes angry if I say I'm not going. I don't know what to do."

Although not exclusive to stepfamilies, this situation frequently occurs after the blend. Learning how to respond lovingly is no easy task. The first step is NOT to react immediately. This is where texting can get us into big trouble. Snarky retaliation or rude responses do not resolve anything. We may feel relief for a few seconds, but the results are typically not helpful. It's easy to be a keyboard warrior and type things we would never say to someone's face. The opposite is also true. Becoming a doormat and allowing people to treat us badly isn't healthy. Discovering how to handle situations like Michaela's may take time and resources. To learn how to handle a verbal, physical, emotional, or spiritual assault from another person, I highly recommend the resource *The Emotionally Destructive Relationship* by Leslie Vernick.

She shares, "Because we are all sinners, we are all capable of doing hurtful things to each other. What makes certain actions sinful and destructive is their repetitive pattern, as well as a lack of awareness, lack of remorse, and lack of significant change. This distinction should not minimize the sinfulness and destructiveness of isolated incidences. There are times when a single incident of abuse or serious deceit is all it takes to completely destroy your relationship; even if the offender is remorseful and desires to change, it only takes one bullet to kill someone. If you are in a relationship that lacks mutual caring, safety, honesty, or respect, and you regularly feel anxiety, fear, shame, anger, or despair then your emotions are warning you that you are in a destructive relationship, even if you sometimes experience positive feelings towards this person, and are able to have good times together, chronic dread, fear, anger, or stress quench whatever positive feelings you have."[14]

This subject is too complicated to address in a single chapter. However, it's wise to note that Jesus said no to people and walked away from toxic situations all the time. It is not unloving, unkind, or unchristian to station a safeguard to protect your heart, mind, body, and soul.

Here's a brief checklist that might help to determine if you are an enabler or a people pleaser.

Do you:

- Feel guilty saying no?
- Have a sense of dread, fear, or anger if you are not in control of a situation?
- Desire to solve other people's problems?
- Make excuses for the destructive behavior of those you love?
- Fear retaliation or the removal of love if you are non-compliant?
- Allow people to speak to you in a disrespectful or critical manner?

---

[14] The Emotionally Destructive Relationship, Leslie Vernick, Harvest House Publishers, 2007, p 28

- Desire to avoid problems at all costs, believing that no conflict will help the situation?
- Have the belief that rescuing another person from poor choices is Christlike?
- Allow guilt or shame to minimize the behavior of others? Phrases such as, "It's not that bad" ruminate in your mind.
- Pervert Bible verses about love and mercy as an excuse to tolerate the behavior?
- Believe that walking on eggshells, or constant drama, is a normal way to live?

Michaela isn't helping her husband, family, or stepfamily by ignoring the in-laws' behavior—she is harming them. She isn't earning respect or love; she is creating disdain. And she is sabotaging her husband's responsibilities. He should be defending his wife and addressing the behavior of his family members and kids.

It is his job to ensure his children aren't treating his wife with disrespect and disdain. Her need to please is getting in the way of godliness.

Once we understand that we are harming our loved ones by overlooking, ignoring, and tolerating their bad behavior and choices, we see into the mind of Christ. Jesus is the only rescuer with the right motives.

Typically, people rescue other people because it meets a need in us. It's done to relieve a selfish motive, even if it appears godly.

Michaela doesn't want her in-laws to dislike her. So, she is attempting to win them and her husband's favor with the only method she knows. She gives them whatever they demand of her.

Once we understand that we are harming our loved ones by overlooking, ignoring, and tolerating their bad deeds, we obtain the mind of Christ.

God explains it this way.

Before I was afflicted, I went astray, but now I obey your word. Psalm 119:67

The psalmist reveals how his pain is a consequence of a decision to sin. And the pain is what finally taught him to stop. His choice to change his actions turned him around and healed the pain. Without a consequence, the sin continues.

God has no problem allowing us to suffer a consequence for our sin because He knows it's often the only way we will stop. Setting a healthy, loving boundary shouldn't be done with vengeance, spite, or cruelty as the motive. It guards our hearts, minds, spirits, and bodies so that the results might improve.

Learning to let go of enabling behavior is not an easy task. Especially if we learned the behavior early on as a child. Overcoming typically requires help from others. This is especially true in stepfamilies because the dynamics and relationships are often radically different than in biological families.

Here are some very basic steps to start setting healthy, godly, loving boundaries.

- Assess the why. If you were raised in a complex, addiction, controlling, negligent, or abusive home, it will be much harder to diagnose a toxic relationship.
- Understand the patterns. Most destructive relationships follow a blueprint. Leslie's book, or others like

it, can help to discern whether a relationship is truly destructive.

- Learn what to do. Allowing the destruction to continue is not love. It's sin. When we allow and enable a person to treat us inappropriately, we say what they do is acceptable.
- Discover what not to do. You cannot control the actions of another person. No matter how much you desire them to change. No amount of begging, threatening, pleading, or manipulating will cause another person to do what you want. God gives us free will, even if that causes self-destruction.
- Tell someone you trust. Several years ago, I wrote an article called the 12 Traits of an Abuser for Crosswalk.com. My years in divorce recovery ministry taught me how to discern this issue. It was their #8 most-read article for the entire year. Christians are desperate for teaching on this subject and rarely get it in their church. Often, a pastor has no training or understanding on the impact of emotional abuse. Seek a person who has overcome the issue.
- Join Support. Fortunately, there are now excellent Christian support systems and resources for men and women who desire to be set free from Satan's lies about destructive relationships and marriages. For many years, Christians didn't have biblical resources on these subjects. Two excellent ones are Conquer, hosted by Leslie Vernick www.LeslieVernick.com, and Celebrate Recovery www.CelebrateRecovery.com,
- Find a circle. In 2020, Covid caused many people to retreat into a small shell of isolation. Many never came out of it. The Internet is a deceptive

way for those in isolation to mistakenly believe they have community. They do not. They have an impersonal, detached, plastic screen that gives the fake illusion of relationships. God created us to be with other people because we need them, and they need us. This is one of His fundamental ways of healing us.

In case you still don't have confidence in the seriousness of allowing a person to be emotionally abused, perhaps Leslie's explanation can help.

"Emotional abuse, systematically, degrades, diminishes, and can eventually destroy the personhood of the abused most people describe emotional abuse as being far more painful and traumatic than physical abuse. One only has to read reports of prisoners of war to begin to understand the traumatic effects of psychological warfare using emotionally abusive tactics, and this is when the behavior is perpetrated by one's own enemy. When abuse of behavior is perpetrated by someone who promised to love and cherish you, it's even more devastating and destructive."[15]

God does not expect you to ignore, endure, or disregard abuse. Was Jesus abused? Yes. However, he never condoned or ignored it.

Sometimes, He fled.
Sometimes, He tried to reason with the person.
Sometimes, He spoke back.
Sometimes, He implemented a consequence.
Always, He remained holy.

---

15 The Emotionally Destructive Marriage, Leslie Vernick, Waterbrook, 2013 p 11

Shouldn't We be Reconciled?

Jesus forgave his family at the cross. However, he wasn't reconciled to his stepfamily until after the resurrection. It's key to note that they played a role in the restoration.

"Scripture teaches that if there is genuine fruit of repentance, there ought to be some kind of reconciliation. The body of Christ is described as a family. If someone is truly repentant for their sin, can we begin to see and treat this person as a family member (brother or sister) rather than an outcast or enemy? I hope so. I think this is what Jesus wants for his church when he says, Leave your offering to me and go be reconciled to your brother or sister first.

However, this next truth is critical to also accept. Forgiveness doesn't necessarily erase the impact or consequences of sin. Sometimes sin has serious life-long consequences, even when forgiveness is generously given. If you kill someone while driving distracted or reckless or drunk, you can be sincerely repentant, never repeat that behavior, and the person you killed stays dead. Even if the family of the victim forgives you, you may still lose your driver's license or go to prison." [16]

We read that Jesus's half-siblings woke up. They repented. Observing your brother resurrected from the dead tends to do that. They respectfully submitted to be reconciled.

Can Michaela be reconciled with her in-laws? There is no cookie cutter answer when responding to destructive or vicious people. That's why Leslie Vernick has two books on the subject. It's complicated. What is evident in her situation is how her husband doesn't understand the severity of the impact it's having on his wife.

---

16 Leslie Vernick, blog, Forgiveness and Reconciliation—What's the difference?

A few brief steps:

First, pray. "God give me wisdom and discernment in this situation. Help me to see it through your eyes and not my own. Teach me to respond as Jesus would."

Second, she needs to calmly speak with her husband and clearly explain how this is affecting her and the action steps she is taking to stop it.

Third, she must sit with an objective person. Avoid anyone who is emotionally attached to the situation. This usually includes family.

Fourth, if she can't set healthy boundaries on her own (most people don't naturally know how), she needs a therapist or group to teach her what steps to take.

Fifth, calmly, rationally, and peacefully follow through with setting the godly boundaries even if the in-laws, including her husband, are angry.

Loving and responding like Jesus is not easy. Fortunately, God doesn't expect us to do it with our own strength. It's the Holy Spirit's job to fill, teach, and guide us on how to respond as Jesus would. Frequently, our problem is that we have received teachings on this subject that are not biblically accurate. We have been taught that loving like Christ means ignoring sin.

Nothing could be further from the truth.

WHAT DO WE LEARN FROM THIS STEPFAMILY?

- Jesus knows what it's like to be rejected by family and stepfamily
- Jesus's stepdad was a good and honorable man. He remained engaged to Mary even when being pregnant could have gotten her stoned to death. It was

also a humiliation for him. This took tremendous courage.
- Scripture isn't afraid to speak the truth about family. It reveals how cruel Jesus's stepfamily was to Him.
- Jesus can teach us how to live in the perfect balance between truth and grace.
- Setting healthy, godly boundaries isn't an easy task to be taken lightly. Jesus is our example.
- Forgiveness is available if we learn the holy how.
- We can forgive someone and not be reconciled to them if they are not repentant.

HOW DOES LEARNING ABOUT *THIS* STEPFAMILY STRENGTHEN *MY* STEPFAMILY?

- Honestly evaluate your home. Are you or your spouse being harmed or abused by people in the family? How about in-laws or extended family?
- Do you struggle to set boundaries? Have you discovered the root causes?
- If your spouse refuses to acknowledge the pain and hurt in your home, what action steps are you willing to take?
- Has someone taught you that forgiveness means ignoring, tolerating, or minimizing the pain caused by others? What would life be like if you learned the holy definition of forgiveness?
- Where can you go to learn what it looks like to live, love, forgive, and reconcile in a godly manner with others?
- Are you able to say no to those in your family? Are you fearful of the consequences if you say no? Do you fear the loss of love and relationship if you

don't comply? Did you know that is a sign of abusive behavior?
- Are you a bully? Have you asked God to reveal if you are the one causing pain in your home? Do you treat family members with respect? Would your family members agree with your perspective? Are you willing to ask and hear the opinions from those in your family, including your kids and spouse? What steps will you take to change?

PRAYER

Dear Lord, I need help. I'm confused. And I know you are not a God of confusion. Help me to understand the truth about forgiveness. I realize that my childhood may have damaged my ability to have healthy relationships. I need to walk in the freedom that you died to give me. I need to be untangled from the excruciating complexities that keep my mind wrapped in doubt, discouragement, fear, and loneliness. You paid too much for me that I should live in this despair. Holy Spirit, I need your light to guide me towards freedom. And Lord, show me when I'm the perpetrator. Teach me when I'm the abuser. Reveal the areas in my life where I am being cruel, hurtful, or abrasive. It is the desire of my heart to be holy as you are holy. I believe you can teach me if I surrender to your ways and not my emotions. I trust you, Lord. I know you can do it. I love you, Lord. Amen.

~ 9 ~
BIOLOGICAL FAMILY VS. BLENDED FAMILY
Digging Deeper into the Differences

Many people think that stepfamilies should, and can, function the same way as a first-time family.

A big part of my job is educating individuals, pastors and church leaders on why blended families are extremely different than biological families.

Statistics reveal that the number of those who remarried, recoupled, or created a stepfamily is increasing daily. These families need help because they divorce at higher rates than first-time marriages. They need to know that another divorce isn't the only answer.

Pastors often ask me why blended families can't use the same resources designed for first-time marriage. It's easy to answer. If a person hasn't experienced blending two families, they assume everyone will unite, love, mix, and meld together easily. But that's incorrect. The dynamics and emotions of a blended family are radically more complicated.

Therefore, if the goal is for the marriage to survive and thrive, it's crucial for people to discover and embrace the

Child Attachments

Biological Parents	Stepparents
Quick to offer grace in conflict. Children have a high tolerance for conflict and disappointment.	Low tolerance for conflict, easily angered and offended, capable of turning against.
"Insider" status. Children view parents as "part of the club" with all the rights and privileges of membership.	"Outsider" status. Viewed with a "you don't belong" attitude and a "you-have-to-earn-the-right-to-membership" status. If an insider (sibling, biological parent, extended family member) has a conflict with the stepparent, the insider will likely be supported and judged "right."
Auto-love. Love for the biological parent isn't decided, it's automatic and deeply felt.	Decision-love. Love must be created, nurtured, developed over time, and ultimately decided.
Auto-approval. This attitude says, "If Dad says it, it must be right," and results in a natural bias towards you. It gives the benefit of the doubt and seeks to justify why you are worthy of love (even if acting immorally or irresponsibly).	Decision-approval. Evaluates the stepparent to determine if they are worthy of approval. Is capable of rejection when in doubt.
Auto-trust. It is assumed that you can be trusted (even when proven otherwise).	Decision-trust. Trust is developed over time after the stepparent proves they have goodwill toward the child.
"My space is your space." This attitude says, "What's mine is your: you have permission to enter my personal space."	"My space is mine." This attitude says, "Stepping into my space is a violation

Copyright, The Smart Stepmom, Ron L. Deal and Laura Petherbridge dynamics that are fundamentally and profoundly different in a blended family. This doesn't imply that biological families are better or holier. It does mean biological families (first-time families) function more smoothly.

The child attachment chart reveals some of the key reasons and ways that biological family and stepfamily are vastly different. The essential variance is this: the biological parent automatically possesses a level of trust, love, and grace from their child. The stepparent earns this over time. It isn't instant. A parent is essential to their child. A stepparent isn't. Therefore, the child's default posture, even if they are furious with a parent, is one that preserves the relationship with dad or mom at all costs. A child will seek out a parent's approval and love in countless ways (ex: obedience, forgiveness, seeking attention, etc.) On the other hand, a child's relationship with their stepparent (especially in the beginning or if the introduction time was quick) is confusing at best. The child questions everything, including, "Do I even want you to be there for me?" Or "Will loving you cost me the connection with my other biological parent or others?" A common response to this confusion is for the child to act out with disobedience, anger, rejection, and accusations."[17]

In other words, in a child's mind, the parent isn't viewed as expendable. A stepparent is a variable. While this may hurt a stepparent, and it is difficult to embrace, understanding the why beneath the nonessential attitude should bring relief. It's not about the stepparent; it is the role they represent in the child's life.

The adults label the stepparent as "another parent," not the child. The adults desperately want to create another

---

[17] The Smart Stepmom, Deal and Petherbridge, Bethany House, 2009, p. 142-143

"instafamily," and the child is punished if their emotions don't line up.

Our society has made this more difficult. We currently promote and advertise that a stepparent is the same as a biological parent. If I had a dollar for every well-meaning parent or stepparent who said to me, "We don't use the word 'step' in our home," I'd be rich. The tasks and roles for these two people may be the same. However, it doesn't mean the bond and relationship are equal. Pushing and promoting the "same as a parent" framework and pacifying stepparents with the belief that they fill the same role as the biological parent sets them up for disappointment, anger, sorrow, and resentment if the child doesn't feel the same. Some kids never attach, or embrace, a stepparent. Some kids attach immediately.

Therefore, if the goal is for the marriage to survive and thrive, it's crucial for the adults to discover and embrace the dynamics that are fundamentally and profoundly different in a blended family. This doesn't imply that biological families are better or holier. It does mean biological, nuclear families (first-time families) function more smoothly and have fewer hurdles to overcome.

Here's why:

- Stepfamilies are birthed upon loss: a death, divorce, or uncoupling of the original biological family has occurred. A stepfamily can't form without it. Underneath the stepfamily unit are the fractured memories, emotions, and grief of this former family. These broken pieces can be healed, but they require time and often professional help. Blended families are often very resistant to embracing this truth. However, a refusal to acknowledge the issues prolongs the healthy formation of the new blend.

- Everyone is grieving and healing at different stages. Usually, everyone hates it when I share this. They refuse to believe there is lingering pain. At the time of the remarriage, the adults are typically more healed than the children. The brain of a child is not yet fully developed. If parents assume their child has fully mended, when they have not, the unresolved loss and grief will resurrect itself at some point in the future.
- Multiple faces in the family photo. A stepfamily typically includes many more people than a biological family. My co-author friend, Ron Deal, likes to say, "instead of a family tree—you have a family forest." The addition of new in-laws, stepsiblings, grandparents, cousins, and extended family significantly increases the potential for conflict. And each family member is entering the newly formed blend with a different set of expectations, dreams, and emotions.
- There are gains and losses. The adults in the blend view the new marriage as a beautiful, fresh restart at life. The darkness of death or divorce is over, and now the sun is shining and bringing happiness. However, the children's perspective of this new family may be different. No matter their ages, the kids may view the stepparent as an interloper. To the child, their safety and security are once again shaken. This triggers a fear of losing the parent to the new relationship.
- Blending everyone takes time. In their excitement, the remarried couple frequently assumes that everyone will get along and relate like siblings within a few months. The passion to recreate the feelings and connections of a biological family is common. Unfortunately, bringing everyone under one roof in

harmony is typically not an overnight experience. If the couple does their research and attends premarital classes geared for stepfamilies, they have a better chance of overcoming the complexities that may occur.

- Discovering unmet expectations is a common experience upon entering a stepfamily. Stepfamilies want to look, act, think, respond, and relate like biological families. And that can occur. But if the "instafamily" dream bubble bursts, and the people inside the home don't meet the needs a person has for love, family, community, and connection, it can be painful. It's wise to lower the expectations and allow the relationships to occur naturally.
- The most significant stressor in stepfamilies is parenting styles. Parenting is one of the most important discussions a couple can have before blending. Couples assume they have a plan, but it's rarely the case. A child does not automatically view a stepparent as a parent because of a wedding ring on their parent's finger. The attachment between a parent and child is a unique hard-wired bond. It is unrealistic to expect the stepparent or the child to have that instantaneous connection with someone other than their mother, father, sibling, or grandparent.
- Coparenting. Perhaps the biggest difference between a biological family and a stepfamily is that the children live in two homes. It's not uncommon for these homes to have drastically different and often opposing views on morals, discipline styles, faith, belief systems, cleaning chores, eating preferences, spending habits, etc. As the children observe the vast differences between life at dad's house and life at mom's, a

confusing and sometimes chaotic existence begins. A wise parent creates a unified co-parenting plan. This includes accepting that one parent cannot control what goes on in the other home unless it is illegal. It's the easiest, most cohesive situation when the two homes can work in harmony. It requires both biological parents to desire what is best for the children, which can be challenging after a divorce.

It can be exhausting. Sometimes, the stress can seem too powerful to bear. God understands. And He reminds us that we are not alone. We are not doomed. God offers help to unravel the things that so easily entangle us. He wants us to learn how to overcome the traps that hiss, ridicule, and attack. The attacks attempt to take us down and destroy our family.

What to Do When the Kids Don't Embrace a Stepsibling or Half-Sibling

A few years ago, I was in an airport waiting on a flight, and two women were sitting behind me, discussing family.

"You know my son, Randy, just remarried," the first woman shared.

"Yes, I remember. How is it going?" the second responded.

"Terrible. My grandkids and Jessica's kids don't get along at all. They fight constantly," she replied.

"Randy just can't understand it, and neither do I. They got along great before the wedding. When Jessica's kids weren't around, they would beg Randy to bring them to her house. Now they can't stand being around each other without WW3 happening."

"Wow, that's so strange! Did something happen?" lady number two inquired.

"No, it just suddenly shifted after the wedding. When they got home from their honeymoon, Randy explained to the kids that they are one family now and how Jessica's kids became their brothers and sisters. Afterward, the kids became furious, stomping through the house and slamming doors. They refuse to accept it. One of my grandsons shouted, "He's not my brother. I want to go live with my mom," and stormed off. I don't know what has gotten into them."

I do.

I resisted the urge to turn around and share a lesson on stepfamily dynamics with these two women. I'm proud of my restraint. In general, people want to believe the "happily ever after" of a stepfamily. They don't want to know why stepfamily dynamics are different and complicated and require a diverse approach. It bursts the romance bubble. It's easier to blame the kids and label them as miserable, self-absorbed, or bipolar.

Educating the Family

A big part of creating a healthy blended family is knowing how to educate the extended family and relatives.

In the scenario above, grandma needs a crash course on stepfamily nuances. She needs a deep dive into why her grandson changed and the emotions behind his statement of rebellion and refusal.

Let's begin with some statistics.

"In the last two decades the family landscape has evolved to include cohabitating stepfamilies which have become a central part of U.S. families, with an estimated 40% of American children growing up in cohabitating household by age 12 (Manning, 2015)

According to the Pew Research Center, 42% of American adults have at least a step or half relative in their family, whether a stepparent, a step or half-sibling, or a stepchild (Pew Research, 2011). Remarriage is currently on the rise; in 2013, 20% of new marriages were between people who had both previously been married at least once compared to 13% in 1980. More so, 23% of married adults (in 2013) had been married before (Pew Research, 2014). This leads to a growing number of children who spend their childhood as members of stepfamilies. The traditional family setup of children raised by both biological parents in the U.S. has declined since the 1960s. In 1960, 73% of American children lived in intact families – with both biological parents. However, this has reduced to 46% in 2014 (Pew Research, 2015). Of the 64.8 million children under 18 in 2010, 4% were estimated to live with a stepparent (Kreider & Lofquist, 2014).

When a couple remarries after a former spouse's death or divorce, they are thrilled to begin again with a new love. Parents frequently expect their children, young or old, to feel the same way as they do.

There's the rub.

"My wife died a few years ago, and I thought my life was over. After her death, I was in deep grief, and I became much closer to my adult kids," Stanley stated. "Then I met Samantha. We instantly connected and fell madly in love and married six months later. I assumed my kids would be thrilled, but they aren't. They don't come around anymore, and the new bond we formed after their mom's death seems to have disappeared. I don't understand why they don't want me to be happy."

Stanley only sees this through his personal lens. Not the perspective of his kids. If he genuinely wants to rekindle the bond with his children, he must hold off on the expectation that they will embrace Samantha with open arms.

What about a stepparent who has been involved with the child since they were little? Surely, that child loves the stepparent the same way they do a biological parent, right?

When Stepkids Step Away

"My stepson asked me not to attend his graduation. He says he only wants his biological family to attend", stepdad Craig stated. "I've been in this kid's life since he was seven years old. I did everything a father would do and paid for most of it. And *now* I'm no longer family? He's behaving like a self-centered brat, and I'm furious with him."

"My stepdaughter, Britney, just had her first baby", stepmom Kari shared. "She was four years old when her mom left. I married her dad one year later and became her full-time mom," she continued.

"Her mother came back into Britney's life two years ago, and now she barely connects with me. I wasn't invited to be at the hospital when the baby was born or when she brought her home. Her mom, who never showed up for anything when she was a kid, has been by her side the entire time. I am devastated and so angry with myself for being such a fool. I spent time, money, and effort on a child who is rejecting me. I don't understand what I did wrong or how she could toss me aside after all the sacrifices I made for her. I loved and cared for my husband's child as if she were my own. My resentment is growing, and I don't know how to stop it."

Many stepparents, even full-time stepparents, don't realize that when that child becomes an adult, they might push them out of the family circle. And it's more common than people realize.

As a child, they didn't have a choice about being in a stepfamily. But now, as an adult, they do.

I often share that becoming a stepmom has taught me more about how to love like Jesus than any other experience in my life. It's sacrificial. It's often rejection. And it must be done with no expectations for anything in return. Bitterness can take root if I expect my stepfamily to love me in return.

To overcome a soul-deep stepparent rejection and resist the temptation to retaliate, four steps are required:

Step One: Go Deeper

- The desire to understand the why beneath the behavior is the key to starting the process. It's often as simple as the natural desire for a child to draw closer to a biological parent. This is particularly true if the child was young, and the parent abandoned the child or has been absent. In our mind, this child should be angry with the lost parent even if they are now an adult. We want him/her to reject the one who caused them pain. And some do.

    But, more often than not, if that parent reappears, they allow that parent full access to their heart and lives. We logically think the child should be lavishing that praise and relationship onto the stepparent. The one who sacrificially stepped up and became responsible, caring, and compassionate. The one who stepped up when the parent stepped out. That logical thinking comes from a developed, healthy adult brain. It is not the thought process of a child who has been rejected by a parent. When a child suffers trauma, such as the abandonment or death of a parent, a child often has embedded lies of shame, fear, and anxiety. If the child hasn't gotten the proper help, he/she has a brain that is repeating shameful accusations such as, "I'm so unlovable my parent didn't want me. I'm so horrible my parent left me. I'm so despicable even my own flesh didn't choose me" brain. If the adult child never received help to discover how and why the parent's neglect or death affected them, it may reveal itself in destructive ways and other areas of life. Stepparent, you are blaming the wrong person. It's not the child's fault. It's the parent who discarded, died, or neglected the child. To some degree, it's also the fault of the other biological parent, your spouse, if they didn't obtain the help they needed. Dads often don't think the child needs help if he remarries and replaces the lost mom with a new mom. Even with the proper therapy, given the opportunity, a child will often gravitate to a parent who abandoned or left them. Stepparents, it's natural to be hurt and angry with a stepchild if they are pushing you outside the family circle. It's discovering what God would have us do with the anger that poses the greatest question.

In Stanley's situation, where mom has died, there is still the need to get to the bottom of the emotions. It could be the child doesn't like seeing dad with another women, it wounds the memory of the mother. Or maybe dad seems happier with his new wife than he did their mom. The parent must not become demanding or defensive but rather discover the why.

Step Two: Recognize

- Recognize. In many instances, the rejection and snub from a child has very little to do with the actions or presence of a stepparent. The adult child isn't purposely rejecting the stepparent, especially if the person was or is good to him/her. They are rebuffing what the stepparent represents. A broken family. A lost parent. A fractured heart.

"For the day I graduate, I want to have one moment to remember. I want to look out in the audience and see my mother and my father together, smiling and watching me walk across the stage to get my diploma. I want to have an instance where I feel like I have a family. Even if it only lasts an hour, or a day, I'd like to feel what it's like not to have parents who hate each other", a stepdaughter shared.

"On my wedding day, I'd like a family photo of me, my new spouse, and my mother and my father. No stepfamily. I just want one captured moment with the two people who created me. It brings comfort to believe that they were happy that I came into the world at some point in my history.

These two adult children don't detest their stepparents. They merely crave a moment of normalcy.

Stepparent, here's where you can shine. Will you give them that gift? Are you willing to step back for a moment, day, or season so that the child can create memories they need and crave? Are you aware that sacrificially stepping back and giving the child what they need, rather than what you want, may be the strongest and widest bridge you can build? It communicates, "I see you. I see your pain. I see your need. And I know I have the power to either make this an awkward, uncomfortable moment which is all about me, or I can give you this gift because I love you."

Step Three: Step Back and Grieve

Sometimes, it's wise for a stepparent to step back and not pester the stepchild to embrace the stepfamily. It is possible to remain at the line of reconciliation while letting your emotions take a break. I liken it to the biblical story of the prodigal son and his dad. Scripture tells us the dad sees his son while he's a long way off. That means he's watching for him and standing ready to run to him. If the stepchild chooses to walk closer to the relationship again, it's wise for him/her to know the stepparent is willing. During that time, a stepparent can send little notes on special occasions, make a favorite cookie, drop off a small gift, etc. These things communicate, "I understand, and I'm here if you desire to reconnect." Let the child move at the pace they desire.

"Our first Christmas together, I was so excited to have all my husband's kids and grandkids over for dinner", Leslie shared. "I spent days and days preparing favorite foods. Their mom/grandmom had died three years previously, and I knew they hadn't had a big meal together like this since she passed. I wanted to lavish them."

"After we said the blessing, they started reminiscing," she continued. "They talked about family vacations, sporting events, and their favorite memories as a family. Quickly, I began to emotionally cower. I felt ostracized and outside the family circle. As they laughed and enjoyed themselves, I was emotionally sinking into despair. And if that wasn't enough, they barely touched my special cranberry salad and sweet potato casserole. Those were always my family's favorite dishes. I didn't belong. I didn't fit in. And I began to get mad."

This family did nothing wrong. They merely had a meal together and talked. It was the stepmom's expectation that got into her mind and began to minimize her value to the family. She had a Norman Rockwell painting in her head; instead, she got a Picasso.

There is no one to blame.

She must embrace that this circle was created before she came along to heal from this. They have no interest in her cranberry salad because they weren't raised with it. Her husband must discover how to draw his new wife into the conversation. Ultimately, she will need to decide if she will give her stepfamily the gift of letting them recollect memories that don't include her. And then create some new stories that do.

Let's be real. Some stepkids will do spiteful things just to upset or aggravate the stepparent.

God will help a stepparent to forgive the child for the hurt they are inflicting. Stepparent grief also occurs during this step. It may be the death of the dream of what the relationship would be with the stepfamily. Remember, it might be for a season or a lifetime. Only God can know and control the future.

The key is to ask God for his perspective.

We are not promised a reward here on earth for what we do for our Father in heaven. It doesn't make the pain and hurt disappear but gives the scar a higher purpose.

Our job as Christian stepparents is to respond as Christ would. Is it easy? No. It's sacrificially hard. It's significantly important if the stepkids aren't followers of Christ. It may be a stepparent's finest evangelical moment when revealing how a person who loves and serves Jesus responds when rejected.

Step Four: Focus Elsewhere

The enemy of our souls would love for a stepchild's rejection to provoke discouragement, depression, retaliation, and resentment. And for stepmom Angela—it worked. "I told my husband, if I can't be the grandma, then he can't be the grandpa. They either include me and let me spend time with the baby, or they don't get him as the grandpa", she shared.

God says that vengeance is His alone. Instead, we have the Holy Spirit's strength to give us the mind of Christ when we have been wounded by another. Hurtful thoughts will come, and it's crucial to take them captive and force the mind to focus on something that is a blessing or holy. If we dwell and ruminate over the rejection, we will be tempted to respond like this woman did.

To clarify, this doesn't mean we should ignore rude, cruel, or abusive behavior from a stepchild. Love does not mean ignoring, dismissing, or tolerating sin. The stepparent may need to set healthy and holy boundaries to protect themselves from the evil arrows of a disgruntled stepchild. God does not expect, or desire, for us to stand in the line of fire when a person is spewing hate towards us. It's wise to step away and take shelter. Jesus said no to people all the time. However, many of us have not learned how to set boundaries in a godly manner. This will be the perfect time to learn.

Stepparenting isn't for the faint of heart. And it's not for the weak in Christ, either. God will help you. My friend, ministry leader, and author Summer Butler shares how God revealed her role as a stepmom: "You are not raising these children so that they grow up and call you their mother. You are raising them to grow up and call me their Father."

Wow! Powerful.

God is more than willing to give any stepparent the ability to live, respond, and dwell above the pain. We never know what relationships God is using for His glory. And when we love as Jesus does, unconditionally, we leave and trust the results with Him. As stepkids get older, they circle back many times and say, "Thank you." They acknowledge that the road in the relationship has been bumpy, and they apologize. There can be peace and a good connection if the stepparent accepts how it may be different than he/she planned.

HOW DOES THIS STRENGTHEN MY STEPFAMILY?

- What is your greatest source of stepfamily frustration?
- Has God placed you in this stepchild's life for a season or a lifetime?
- If God and my spouse are the only ones who ever recognize all the sacrifices I make for his/her kids, is it enough?
- If being a stepparent isn't what I had hoped it to be, have I grieved the death of that dream? Can I embrace reality?
- Consider why receiving recognition, acknowledgment, or praise for doing what you have done is so important for you.
- Biological Parent: Do you praise your spouse for the hard work they offer to your kids? Why? Why not?
- Does being a stepparent trigger past emotional pain? What are you doing to heal?
- Have you discovered what healthy boundaries are needed? Do you allow your spouse to set healthy boundaries with your children?
- Did you have a stepparent in your life? What do you wish you could tell them?
- What are practical steps you can take to let go of unrealistic expectations?

PRAYER

My Patient Papa,

I thought being a child of divorce had taught me what being in a stepfamily was all about. I was wrong. Very wrong. There are so many emotions, and circumstances that make it different for each child. As a stepmom my motives were right, but my methods weren't always what my stepfamily needed. I've asked them to forgive me, I also ask You to forgive me, too. Kids living in two homes have numerous emotions and thoughts that I didn't understand until now. Holy Spirit, from this moment on nudge me to listen more closely. Prick my heart when I need to learn something new about my blended family. I'm asking. I want to know. Your word in Jeremiah 33:3 tells me to, "Call to me and I will answer you and tell you great and unsearchable things you do not know." I'm calling, Lord. I'm listening. I'm teachable. Thank you for your gentle, calm, and profound wisdom. Amen

~ 10 ~
Adding an "Ours" Baby

When a remarriage occurs, the decision whether to add more children can be complex. Today's stepfamily often faces many of the same emotions and dilemmas when considering the addition of an "ours" baby. Our biblical friends may have faced distinctive cultural challenges, but enlarging today's blended family circle comes with its own set of hurdles.

Stepmom, Heidi Farrell, founder of Not Just a Stepmom, shares her journey.

> "Like many stepmoms, I loved my new stepkids, but I longed for a baby of my own. My husband and I were ecstatic when we found out I was pregnant with an ours baby within the first year of marriage," Heidi explained.
>
> "The announcement to his kids didn't go as we had hoped. It was heart-wrenching to see my stepkids sitting across the table from us with tears in their eyes. They were clearly not happy about the news of a new baby in the family.
>
> "Stepfamily life often happen in a backwards order that can easily throw everyone for a loop. For example, telling a 12 and 9-year-old that they would be getting a new sibling. Then just hoping the news would somehow be welcomed

with delight after their world had already seen some drastic changes.

"Consequently, the whole thing left me with a hollow feeling. It felt terrible to know that I had played a role in hurting them so deeply. I tried to hide my sadness, but inwardly I was crushed" Heidi mourned.

"Not only was I feeling sad and defeated, but my husband was also devastated to have hurt his children. We understood why they reacted the way they did and didn't fault or condemn them for their feelings. Clearly, they had already gone through so much change. Their parents had divorced; then dad got remarried and they acquired a new stepmom. Now they were getting the news of a baby entering the family.

Frankly, they didn't want any more changes.

"Logically we knew that once they got used to the idea, they would be okay. Yet, we had held onto the hope that just maybe they would have shared a tiny piece of our happiness."

Heidi's stepchildren are grown, and they have a good relationship with their half-siblings. But the road wasn't always easy.

Let's join another one of our biblical "ours" babies and see what we can learn from them.

Isaac

He's the one Sarah and Abraham have long awaited. The precious one.

Even though I worked obstetrics and gynecology for three years, do not ask me how Sarah got pregnant in her old age. Ask your pastor. It's a God thing.

They miraculously got the long-awaited ours baby which God had promised.

But as the child grows up alongside his older half-brother Ishmael, Sarah witnesses Ishmael teasing young Isaac. It triggers revenge.

> *One day, Sarah noticed Hagar's son Ishmael playing, and she said to Abraham, "Get rid of that Egyptian slave woman and her son! I don't want him to inherit anything. It should all go to my son."* Genesis 21:9-10

And although Abraham is deeply troubled, he does as she requests.

This is not an uncommon scenario in stepfamilies when an ours baby is added. The biological parent, particularly the mom of the ours baby, watches the half-siblings and/or step-siblings like a hawk. She's looking for any antagonistic actions that display resentment. A biological parent would view sibling fighting and taunting as mischievous teasing or harmless annoyance. But a hyper-vigilant stepmom protecting the ours baby interprets the stepchild's behavior as viciousness towards her child. As Sarah did.

Sometimes the stepmom is right. The stepchild does resent the new baby and intentionally hurts him/her. In other circumstances, it is normal sibling behavior.

The caution for the stepparent is to heed the warning and guard the heart from viewing your child as better, superior, and favored. It's tough to do because stepkids often have unpleasant behaviors.

Mom or dad may be genuinely protecting the ours baby from rough, playful step or half-siblings. But the stepchildren view it as favoritism.

When there is resentment, it's common for older kids to view the ours baby as being treated differently and prized.

The parents will tell you it's not true. However, perception is reality for the person who views it that way.

"My stepsons told me they are upset that we have more pictures displayed of the 'ours' baby than we have of them. I counted them. There are fewer pictures of my own child. But they still believe we favor the 'ours' baby."

In Sarah's situation, she didn't hide her disdain for Ismael and his mother. She has her own family now and doesn't want the reminder of her husband's other child. And it places Abraham in a bad spot. Dads genuinely struggle in this situation as they love both kids. They must come together as a couple and work through the differences.

There are other issues to consider as well.

My own father had a son with his second wife, my first stepmother. I had two stepmoms.

I was 17 when my half-brother was born, so there is an age gap. My dad and his second wife divorced when my half-brother was around eight. I didn't see much of him after that. We have no relationship at this point—his choice.

My father died in 2010. That's the last time I saw my half-brother. His perception of my childhood and visiting my dad and his mother is very different than what my biological brother and I lived. He views our dad very differently than we do because he had a totally different experience with him. I have not tried to convince him otherwise; he firmly believes he's right. I have no hatred towards him, and I pray for him.

In the past, I tried to form a relationship with him but realized it was fruitless. Even though we share the same DNA, I learned to guard my heart and let go. I can't repair the relationship if he has no desire to do the same.

In contrast, I have friends who have half-siblings, and you'd never know they weren't full biological brothers and sisters. They totally embrace each other as family.

We must always remember that the ours baby gets to have the life and family the stepkids crave. The half-sibling lives with both parents in one home, functioning as a unit. This alone can be reason enough to stir hostility or envy. This insight from research done by leading stepfamily experts helps to explain.

"While we can't predict the future, we can anticipate potential outcomes based on research and real-life experiences… One of the key issues half-siblings face when an ours baby arrives is the feeling of displacement. Research by Ganong, Coleman, and Sanner (2020) highlights how half-siblings often experience emotional struggles when a new baby joins the family.

They found that younger "ours" children in stepfamilies often witness the stress their older half-siblings experience during family transitions. Half-siblings may feel overwhelmed by the complexity of the family structure, especially when there is tension between the stepparent and their biological parent. *This can lead to feelings of confusion, frustration, and even guilt.*

Research by Leeuw et al. (2024) indicates that the amount of time half-siblings spend living together significantly affects the closeness of their relationship. Half-siblings who grow up in the same household tend to develop stronger bonds, while those who see each other part-time, often due to custody arrangements, may struggle to connect.

This discrepancy can become more pronounced with the introduction of an ours baby, who shares full-time residence with both biological parents. The lack of shared time between older half-siblings and the new baby can lead to an increased sense of division within the family.

As the 2021 study by Landon, Ganong, and Sanner found, half-siblings who only interact occasionally may feel less responsibility for or attachment to their younger sibling, further complicating family cohesion. While the early stages of welcoming an ours baby can be stressful, the long-term outlook for sibling relationships is not always negative. Donagh et al. (2022) found that over time, many half-siblings adjust to the new family structure and form meaningful bonds with their younger sibling.[18]

Adding an ours baby can be a beautiful experience. It's often the one person in the home that binds everyone together. In our book, *The Smart Stepmom,* Ron Deal and I share an entire chapter on who, when, and why to add an ours baby. We also share healthy and unhealthy motives.

When You Disagree on Adding an Ours Baby

I am amazed at the number of couples who didn't discuss whether to add children before they got married.

Often, the husband is already a dad who doesn't want to add more kids after a remarriage. That's not always the case, but it's the most common scenario. When a woman believes her spouse is refusing to hear her feminine heartbeat, especially if she doesn't have biological kids, or he is unwilling to discuss or have compassion toward her maternal longing, it can be the catalyst for marital disaster.

It's crucial for this discussion to occur before the marriage.

Warning! Ladies, hear me clearly. If your fiancé doesn't want to add kids, or he's highly hesitant—believe him. If he's attempting to pacify your wants to keep you, it won't end well. Do not try to control, manipulate, or deceive him into having a baby.

---

18 https://stepmomcoach.com/a-new-sibling-how-stepchildren-may-feel-about-an-ours-baby/

Men, do not tell your fiancé you are willing to add more children if you aren't. The "I can talk her out of it after we are married" mentality is devious and sinful. Honesty is an obligation. A "bait and switch" behavior can destroy a marriage. The spouse feels deceived, and well they should.

If the couple can't come to an agreement, I advise professional help. Either she will need to accept her husband's decision and lay it to rest. Or the husband will need to agree to have a baby.

And if the couple has not married yet, this decision should be finalized in concrete before saying, "I do."

Understanding the reasons why a man might not want to add more children is vitally important.

Fear

A spouse may struggle with guilt or fear after a divorce. A parent, especially a dad, may feel overwhelmed regarding how adding another baby will affect the relationship with the current children. It's also possible that he/she feels like a parenting failure with his first set of children, and he/she fears a repeat performance.

Money

Babies are expensive. If financial pressures are elevated, and dad pays child support to his first family, he may view the addition of another child as imprudent and reckless. It's extremely important to count the cost of adding another child because dad brought those children into the world and is responsible for caring for their needs. If dad chooses to remarry, he should not be expected to stop providing for his first set of kids. Men and women view failure through a different lens. If a husband feels he is not providing for his family, he will likely resist having another baby.

Kids

A parent often knows that adding another baby will cause friction and perhaps distance with the kids that already exist. And it's not an unreasonable fear. Especially if the ex-spouse is difficult and argumentative. Adding a baby can stir more anger and tension between the homes. If the spouse doesn't want to take that risk, it's a serious problem.

Mighty Mistakes

A huge mistake some women make is to get pregnant purposely after their husband says no. Or she throws such a manipulative tantrum that he finally gives in to her desires. She believes all will be fine once he sees the baby and falls in love. This manipulative scheme usually backfires because the husband feels betrayed and trapped. Conniving and deception erode the marriage foundation, often causing a collapse. Solid relationships are built on honesty, trust, compassion, and compromise.

A second perilous problem is the husband's selfish decision to "bait and switch" the spouse. This occurs when a husband agrees to have a child with his fiancé, knowing she won't marry him otherwise. Then after the wedding, he changes his mind and says no. This leaves her feeling trapped, tricked, and conned. She can't trust his words or his heart towards her. This "gotcha", especially for the Christian who takes the marriage vows very seriously, is a perfect storm for disaster.

Unfortunately, I've coached many stepmoms who said, "This was a deal breaker for me, and he knew it. I would never have married him if I had known he didn't want more children. I'm devastated; I don't know if I can recover from this."

This massive destruction of trust will likely impact the marriage until it is resolved, typically with a professional therapist.

Through the Eyes of the Child

"Laura, my daughter, just told me she no longer feels a part of our family. I'm totally baffled. She said that since my wife and I now have a baby, we are a family, and she no longer feels like she belongs. How can I convince her that the new baby doesn't change anything?"

The new baby might not change anything for the parent and the stepparent. But it is a huge transformation for the stepchild.

Her new half-sibling has everything this daughter wants—an intact family. A mom and dad in the same home, lavishing love over their baby. She doesn't have that. The baby does. In her mind, it creates a family circle that doesn't include her. She goes back and forth between homes. The baby won't. This stepchild has two parents who don't like each other. The baby gets a peaceful, secure, unified home. She used to be the baby in the family, now she's the oldest. It's changed her birth order.

Yes, first-time families sometimes deal with jealousy when adding a new baby. However, everyone is on the same playing field, with the same parents. A biological parent already has a bond with their older child. Plus, when a stepparent, especially a stepmom, has her own child, she instantly experiences something she never had before. Even if she deeply loves her stepchild, the astonishing connection and unconditional love for her own baby is different. It's indescribable. It's normal. It's godly. There is no shame in loving your own flesh and blood in a way that is distinctively different than a stepchild.

As much as we try to convince ourselves and post all over social media that kids aren't and shouldn't be affected by adding an ours baby, it's not true.

Does it mean disaster? No. It means more hard work.

The key is the biological parent. The more time mom or dad invests and pours into his/her child from the first marriage, the less likely the child will feel pushed outside the circle.

What to Consider Before Adding a Baby

- Consider all the factors before automatically adding another child.
- Discuss it with all the kids. They don't get to dictate the decision, but it prepares the parents beforehand.
- Get quiet with God and ask Him to reveal your root motive for adding a baby. Is it for revenge? Is it natural because you desire a child?
- Sometimes, a motive for adding a baby is to compete with the other home. That reason isn't wise, healthy, or kind.
- A baby should never be placed in a situation to "bring everyone together." A new baby shouldn't be viewed as the glue. It's a tremendous burden to place on a child.
- Will you dislike your stepchild if they refuse to bond with an ours baby?
- Can we afford another child? Do I believe the other children should change their current activities and financial support so we can add another baby?

When You Have an Ours Baby

- Has an ours baby taken center stage in the home? If so, what's good or bad about that?

- Have you prepared a will, estate plan, or end-of-life documents? Do they show favoritism to the ours baby? Sometimes, it's necessary to entrust one child more than the other. The heart and motives are the key to this decision.
- Am I willing to listen to my kids or stepkids when they believe there is favoritism? What am I willing to do if this happens?
- It's not uncommon for older kids to show no interest in a new half-sibling. This can make a parent or stepparent very angry. Ask yourself why. Am I willing to let the kids choose whether they want to add this new baby into their lives?
- Many kids and stepkids who ignore a new baby will embrace the child later in life. Let God work on the child's heart. Stop forcing a relationship.
- If you resent your stepkids for making it harder on the ours baby, what will you do with those emotions?

PRAYER

Lord, adding another baby to our home is a big decision. Give us wisdom.

Help me to be open to your guidance and not allow feelings to dictate my actions. If I secretly believe adding a baby will make our marriage better, help me to discard that thinking. If I want a baby to make us more a "normal" family, help me to realize it's unhealthy. Teach me how to see our family and marriage as you do.

A baby is a beautiful gift from you. He or she is also a huge responsibility. Please keep me from resenting my spouse's first set of kids. If finances are an issue, help me to remember that you command my spouse to provide for his/

her kids. Teach me to release any negative thinking that my stepkids should be happy about a new sibling. Adding more children should not be used as a weapon against my stepkids.

Lord, if it's your will that we add a baby, please help us do that in a godly, loving, home. Give us the wisdom and clarity to walk the steps necessary to bring peace into our home. We desire to glorify you with our lives. Amen.

~ 11 ~
STEPFAMILY STEPS TO VICTORY

"We went to a stepfamily seminar, and we read books on how to blend, (well, mostly my wife read the books, I glanced at them). We prepared and thought we understood how to merge our two families," stepdad Jeremy described. "And yet after the wedding we were blind-sided by the numerous issues we face. I won't lie—I'm angry. I don't understand why this is still so complicated five years later."

My heart aches for Jeremy and his wife. The truth is it's exceptionally hard to prepare for, or predict, the outcome of stepfamily living. Part of the difficulty is due to numerous factors demanding consideration and how each situation is unique.

A huge part of the reason why stepfamilies struggle is due to attitude. They are trying to mimic or recreate a biological family. It rarely works.

"I read in several stepfamily resources that it takes approximately seven years for everyone to blend and bond. We are in year nine, and the kids barely speak to each other. I feel cheated. I did the hard work to make this happen, and we don't see positive results," stepmom April shared.

It's not a formula. There is no way to predict how each family member will react in a blend. The wise way to approach a remarriage is to discover the common pitfalls and the areas that often cause conflict and do what is best to solve them.

Here are some of the most common reasons why people like Jeremy and April are ambushed by the continuing complexities of blending a family.

Don't become discouraged. There is hope. Remember, anyone who is willing can discover ways to maneuver challenging situations. The problems might not just disappear, but God always has a way to overcome the stress and move forward in a productive manner. As I write this, I've been a stepmom for nearly thirty-nine years. We still have issues that pop up from time to time.

Read that again. Thirty-nine years. It's normal. Accept it and learn how to navigate.

These are common reasons why stepfamilies struggle.

- Losses

    Stepfamilies are birthed on loss. Remarried couples hate this statement. That doesn't change its validity or pragmatism. A death, divorce, or end of a relationship had to occur for the newly formed family to exist. And with loss comes an array of emotions to compound the situation, such as sadness, anger, fear, and distrust, to name a handful.

    If a couple is unwilling to recognize or denies the losses, they cannot be addressed. It's nearly impossible to move forward, heal, and thrive in the blended family without acknowledging and exploring the "reality of relationships past."

    Common statements like, "I never really loved my former partner (or my spouse didn't love his/her spouse), therefore, it doesn't affect us," is a typical mistake. Denying the previous marriage or relationship does not make the second marriage strong. Ironically, the refusal to consider the hidden emotions, grief, anger, and loss (to the spouse or the children) produces weakness and vulnerability in the current relationship.

Why? A person can't heal from what they refuse to admit, discover, and acknowledge. Even if a baby resulted from a one-night stand, there are different losses to be considered.

- The kids are struggling more than we realized.

Parents and stepparents also hate this statement. I'm sorry.

When a child hurts, a parent grieves. And if mom or dad made a choice that is the root reason for the child's pain, tremendous guilt may follow. Even when the other parent is the culprit for the heartache, watching a child suffer is extremely painful—and shameful. So, they refuse. The opposite is also true. Some parents have been lulled into believing a lie that "the kids will be fine." They are unwilling to accept how the divorce or death has affected their kids. Society and Hollywood fuel this flawed, inaccurate, detrimental perspective. Not long ago, I commented on a stepmom's Facebook page regarding the pain kids experience when their parents divorce. I was shocked at the vitriol spewed back at me. Numerous women savagely attacked me and brutally replied that I was dead wrong. They sincerely believed, and had convinced themselves, that stepkids don't suffer at all. That divorce doesn't affect kids negatively at all, and that they are lucky to have stepparents. No number of statistics or expert quotes to the contrary could sway them into even considering they might be wrong. Just because we believe something, or it is popular on social media, doesn't make it factual.

Any honest therapist, counselor, or divorce recovery expert, Christian or not, will agree. The loss of the original family by divorce, death, or a breakup is devastating for a child. It embeds fear, uncertainty, anger, and sadness deep within the child. As children feel out of control, they worry about when the next bad thing will happen. The child isn't doomed to become a serial killer, but they have emotions that need to be addressed.

Accepting the truth and seeking help for the child brings restoration and peace. I'm not suggesting a parent should lose hope or live in humiliation. I'm simply stating a parent will be unable to help a child heal until they are willing to acknowledge the child's emotions.

- Common Mystery

    There is one astounding comment that I repeatedly hear in stepfamily ministry. It's regarding the child that was enthusiastic, excited, and happy for mom or dad to remarry. This was mentioned previously, but it's so crucial I'm sharing it again. A child, young or teen, can't wait to live with the new parent, stepbrothers, and/or stepsisters, and then after the "I do," everything changes. This child, eager to have another mom or dad, suddenly becomes irritable, belligerent, and distant.

    What happened?

The wedding.

We think kids don't understand. They do. Sometimes, more than we do. A switch was flipped. And a light in the brain came on. Unexpectedly, the kid most eager to blend has morphed into a monster! Because a child's brain is not yet fully formed and does not have the capability to process events or situations as an adult brain would, they had no way to fully process or grasp what was coming with the new marriage.

Then, right before their eyes the reality becomes apparent.

This sudden insight makes things shockingly clear. His/her young awareness swirls with panicked thoughts of, "No, no—NO!! This isn't what I thought it was going to be. I want to go back to the old way. I want my mommy/daddy back. I'm losing my parent. I'm scared, I don't like this. I hate change. What will happen to me now? This means my real parents can't ever get back together. I'll never have my family back together again. No, no, no. I'm afraid. Make it stop."

Unless the parent and stepparent understand how fear is at the root of the behavior it can feel like a massive rejection of the marriage. And in some ways, it is. Take heart—it's normal and takes time.

As a side note, don't be surprised if this happens with adult kids also. They grieve too.

"My stepdaughter wailed like a baby during our ceremony. You would have thought it was a funeral, not a wedding," stepmom Janelle shares. "I was furious. Why couldn't she control herself? She's a grown woman." She was grieving, stepmom. The death of her biological family was on display, and she wept.

The Process Takes Longer Than We Realized

"Before we got married, I read that it takes seven years for a stepfamily to blend," stepdad Scott remarked. "I thought, that's ridiculous, ours won't take nearly that long. We are in year six, and things are better but not fully settled."

In the generation of fast food, expeditious Amazon, Zoom, rapid communication, and immediate answers, we have difficulty with anything that takes a long time. Especially when the wait is difficult.

Almost every stepfamily expert, Christian and non, will share that forming a healthy, thriving stepfamily takes time. And if the union happened quickly after the couple met, and the kids haven't had time to process the new normal, it takes longer. Accepting this truth will lower the expectations and ease a lot of anguish. And there is no guarantee. "We are in year fifteen, and my stepkids still dislike my kids. I'm not sure they will ever blend," Tiffany shared.

Who's in First Place?

Now it's my turn to reveal a statement and question, I hate. "Laura, who comes first the marriage or the kids?" My answer, "That's impossible to answer because the kids were there first." Putting the marriage first does not necessarily mean putting the kids second. It's complicated. This is one of the most mis understood subjects surrounding stepfamilies. And the Christian struggles the most. We believe in the sanctity of marriage. That's a good thing. And it's easy to explain in a first marriage with no kids involved because we go from single—to married. One stage moves into the next. Then kids are added one at a time chronologically.

But in a remarriage, you get an "Instafamily." Now what?

"My kids have been in first place in my life for the last five years, since my divorce," newly married Shauna revealed.

"They have been through a lot of trauma and loss with the changes that occurred. I had to protect them from numerous situations. How am I supposed to honor my husband and put him ahead of my children? Won't my kids feeling like they have been abandoned?"

Ah-ha! Shauna has asked the "million dollar" stepfamily question.

I strongly recommend that a couple tackle this subject—and define the words—before getting married or remarried. Do not wait until after the ceremony.

It seems simple. And it's true, if the marriage isn't the foundational priority, the home will crumble.

The number one reasons stepfamilies fail is because the biological parent did not factor in, admit, recognize, or learn how to move their child from the front seat to the back seat. And the stepparent has the irrational illusion that putting the marriage first means hurling the stepkids into the trunk.

Putting the marriage first means unity. It means incorporating a cohesive and organized system of parenting and co-parenting. Defining the stepparent's role in the home before the marriage is essential. When we expect our spouse to play a role or not play a part that hasn't been defined and stabilized, it creates chaos. After the biological parent explains the stepparent's role to the kids, he/she must abide by the arrangement. If the biological parent backs down and refuses to stand in unity with a spouse, turmoil erupts.

The dangerous and disastrous temptation for the stepparent is to quickly take over the discipline and "parental control" of a stepchild. They view the parent as lenient and now that they are in the picture, structure will ensue. It is a massive, common mistake.

Not only does this choice backfire, but it can potentially destroy all future relationships with the stepchild. The stepparent cannot parent more than the parent.

NOTE for the fiancé: If your partner currently does not discipline his/her kids, and you disagree with their parenting style, don't get married. Refuse, and run, from the temptation to rescue him or her. Your partner needs to change his/her parenting plan before getting remarried not after. If the stepparent attempts to liberate their spouse from poor parenting choices, the kids will view him/her as the reason the home is no longer fun, easy, relaxed, and comfortable.

Putting the marriage first does not mean putting the kids second. It's a learned process, and it takes time, patience, and a lot of communication.

And it should never mean ignoring or accepting a spouse who treats your child abusively.

The Other Home is Having a Negative Effect on Our Home

Ask most moms or stepmoms about their number one problem concerning blended family living, and they will reply, "The other woman in my home." The new wife and the ex-wife (or stepchild's mom) frequently have a toxic, antagonistic, and confrontational relationship. Sometimes both women are to blame, occasionally it's only one. Regardless, the quarrelsome atmosphere causes tension, instability, and frustration for everyone involved.

I have met horrible ex-wives and wicked stepmoms. The common denominator is the woman refusing to look in the mirror and examine her heart and behavior. She is so focused on blaming the other that she ignores the gasoline she is tossing on the fire. Oftentimes, all it takes is for one of the women to disengage, step back, and stop responding, for the feud will end.

Some men struggle with the biological dad or stepdad too, but it's typically a female frustration within stepfamilies.

Hopefully, this list will reveal that you are not alone in your journey and that what you are experiencing is normal.

God loves your stepfamily. God wants your stepfamily to survive and thrive.

PRAYER

Thank you, Lord, for the wisdom and resource you have given me during season. I'm in awe at what You have revealed. Help me to continue to learn and grow in Your wisdom. Thank you for loving stepfamilies. Help me to be a beacon of Your light, sharing truth wherever I go. Use me to help other blended families. Make me like you, Jesus. Just make me like—YOU! You ARE the ONLY answer. I can't wait to see you face-to-face in heaven. What a perfect and delightful day that will be. Amen.

Appendix

For Moms and Stepmoms

Ladies, I understand. I have worked with stepmoms for over 20 years. I've heard it all. As a stepmom of 39 years, I've lived most of it.

The most common thing stepmoms say to me is, "I had no idea it would be this complicated."

My signature statement is, "Becoming a stepmom taught me more about how to love like Jesus than any other circumstance in my life."

It's often sacrificial, unrewarding, and lonely. However, learning how to love like Jesus can become a beautiful expression of forgiveness, grace, mercy, and peace.

When stepfamily living becomes intense, and a woman feels confused, discouraged, or ambushed, she can become fierce. Hence the phrase, "momma bear."

I like to watch shows such as I Was Prey. It's stories of people who are attacked by an animal and how they survived. In almost every episode, whether it be a bear, giraffe, or another animal (except a shark), it's a female animal that goes ballistic when a human comes too close to her baby. They strike with such force that the human barely survives.

Women can be like that too. Sometimes it's wise; often it's fueled unhealed emotions.

Therefore, I want to address my precious sister stepmoms.

First, I love you. You are my tribe. You have supported me and given me hope, encouragement, wisdom, and laughter more times than I can count.

You have also caused me to weep. When I observe a mom or a stepmom as the one causing the problems in her home—I cry.

We must take a step back and consider whether our actions and behaviors are making the situation better or worse. Our biblical sisters of old provide us with a godly guidance needed to become a woman (mom and stepmom) after God's own heart.

Even when the other home is unpredictable or combative, with God's help and the mind of Christ, our marriage and stepfamily can survive and flourish.

Ladies, lay down your swords.

Here are practical steps that helped me to overcome. It's not easy. But it is possible.

Step One

Stop and rest a minute. Turn off all the noise. Take a deep breath. Often, we can't hear from God because our space has too much commotion. Ask God to clear your mind of negative, antagonistic, anxious, and/or vengeful thoughts. Now imagine the mom or stepmom in your family at the foot of the cross. See her for the first time as a fellow female. What does God see when He looks at her? Are you willing to view her through His eyes? Was she wounded or abandoned as a child? Has she ever asked Him to heal that pain? Does she even know He is capable and longs to do so? When is the last time you prayed for her? When was the last time you forgave her?

I know this is massive. Trust me, I understand how hard it is. Trust Him, He has your BEST in mind.

Step Two

Envision yourself in the other woman's situation. If you are the mom, think of what being a stepmom is like. Consider how hard it is to marry a man who already has kids. Ponder what it's like to be in the middle between the man you love and his children. If you are the stepmom, imagine what it's like to hand your babies, who came from your own body (normally), over to the care of another woman. How frightened she might be that they will enjoy you more or embrace you as a mom.

As soon as your mind starts to wander (and it will—trust me) towards, "My ex doesn't treat me or these kids the way he should" or "I hate that my husband has a child with this woman, I wish she'd move away" stop and take those thoughts captive. Take them hostage and refuse to let them run rampant. Dwelling on what the other woman is or isn't doing correctly won't make your life easier. Allowing anger and frustration to build makes you more stressful, not the other person. Give that situation to God. Lay it down. Only He can change her heart if she is doing something wrong.

Step Three

Focus on what will make the situation better and what will make the situation worse. Think about what is wise rather than, "What are my rights?" Consider, "Will I be the godly one in this relationship, even if she refuses?" Again, I'm not saying you should tolerate abuse, violence, or being insulted. I'm asking, what is your goal? How will you achieve that goal?

Be HONEST and ask yourself, or have a good friend help you to consider:

- Are my responses to the mom/stepmom making life easier for the dad/kids or harder?

- Do dad/kids view me as a person who throws gasoline on the fire or as a peacemaker, (note I didn't say peaceaholic) and someone who attempts to ease stress?
- Do I respond in a way that communicates, "I'm trying my best to respect you," even if the other woman doesn't admit it, or behave that way?
- Have I discovered the difference between setting healthy boundaries and laying down the law because it's my kids/house/rules?
- Do I always assume the mom/stepmom is behind everything that goes wrong with the kids? If you said, "Yes, because she is," that might be true, but it's also a clear indicator that you aren't allowing God to help you see it through her eyes.
- Am I willing to admit that my responses aren't beneficial to my marriage/family/kids/life?
- Am I willing to pray, "Jesus, I need to stop looking for everyone else to change. Lord, change me!"

Step Four

Are you actively involved in a healthy woman's group that helps you to grow as a female, wife, or mom/stepmom? (Do not include social media groups, but an actual growth group.) If not, what is the reason it's not a priority? Who taught you that a productive Christian life could be created independently, without others? Did you know that this thinking is in contradiction to God's perspective?

One of the reasons I've become, and am still becoming, emotionally healthy is because God taught me that I need to be learning from women who are more mature than I am. I weep for younger women who don't know this. And it's a large part of why we are so depressed, anxious, and fearful.

Let me encourage you to take a step to find a good women's group. Many churches offer them. If your church doesn't provide this, look for other churches in your area that might.

Stepfamily living isn't easy, but it can be productive. You can only control your role. You cannot control the woman in the other home. Stop. Say that last sentence out loud. Some days, I'm still learning where I fit into the stepfamily puzzle. But Jesus is the one who knows where I fit. And He's the one who will guide my steps toward harmony if I ask and listen.

It can be done. God will do it through you.

You won't always have harmony, but you can find peace.

Years ago, my husband and I attended my stepson's 45th birthday party. He was eleven when Steve and I married, so we have been in each other's lives for a while.

I decided to make note of the things I did right as a stepmom rather than linger over the things I've done wrong.

Here are a few:

- I Let My Stepsons Love Their Mom

    I know my stepsons love their mom. She is now deceased, but that doesn't change the fact that she brought them into the world, and they have a unique bond. I didn't try to usurp her position even when I disagreed with her choices. To summarize: I give them the freedom to love their mother without fear of hurting me. This was a huge step because I wanted them to love me too. I grew to learn that could happen organically; it can't be forced.

- I Learned How to Set Healthy Boundaries

    As a full-fledged, card-carrying, codependent, it was very hard for me as a stepmom to discern how and when it was necessary to say—NO! This included discovering the difference between a healthy, humble, "No, I won't let you speak to me that way" response as opposed to, "You want to get ugly with me—I'll show you ugly" retaliation. Overcoming the need to please was not an easy task. God had to continuously nudge me to destroy my former way of thinking with His truth. "Laura, that's not your job. That's my job. And I'm big enough to handle your loved ones. Let go."

- I Accept the Things I Can't Control

    My entire world changed once I finally accepted and embraced the revelation that I'll never be able to control the actions of another person. This doesn't mean ignoring or tolerating abuse, it merely means letting go of the distorted perspective that I can manipulate, command, beg or force another person to behave in an intelligent, considerate, or appropriate manner. When my husband's ex-wife chose to speak poorly about me, I learned to let it go. When my stepsons chose to reject or neglect my feelings or requests, I stepped back. I didn't totally disengage, but I stepped back. There is a difference. I've lost count of the times I prayed, "Lord, give me the mind of Christ. I need to think like you rather than like me because it hurts."

- I Admitted My Issues

    Did you ever drive behind a pickup truck loaded to the brim with junk? The debris flies off the flatbed and scatters all over the road. That's how I came into my stepfamily marriage. My heart was filled with putrid, decaying, and emotional garbage placed there long before I met my husband. Before I could become an enjoyable mate or an effective stepmom, I needed surgery on my weary mind and soul. The toxin from past pain must be cleansed and eradicated. It required professional help and time alone with God.

But I chose to do it, and God did His part. Jesus revealed the wounded places from my past that were embedded and affecting my future. I foolishly assumed the pain from my childhood evaporated when I gave my life to Christ and forgave those involved.

I was wrong.

Jesus cleansed my sins but didn't wash away my brain or lingering consequences. My mind needed healing, and it wasn't a light shampoo. It hurt.

- I Got Help for My Distorted View of Marriage

    Children of divorce often have perverted perceptions about marriage. This is especially true when the divorce was tumultuous. I was no exception. Having a single-parent mom who was the original "I am woman, hear me roar" during the 60s and 70s didn't help. It produced confusion and frustration when I attempted to become a wife.

    I had to learn how to communicate, confront, and unify with my husband in a way that benefitted both of us. We attended community groups, read Bible studies, and attended marriage retreats, which strengthened our union.

- I Stopped Preaching and Learned to Love Instead

    I am a Pharisee (a legalist). I am a rule follower. Fortunately, the Holy Spirit pricked my soul with the damage I was doing with this legalism. But not before I was too preachy with Steve's sons. I discovered that my method of sharing about Jesus was doing more to push them away from God than to draw them in. I thought I was sharing the gospel, but I wasn't. I was using it as a weapon to prove I was right.

Being a legalist is much easier than living like Christ. Learning to live and love like Jesus takes time, patience, and a whole lot of the Holy Spirit. That's why so many opt for being a Pharisee instead. Most, like I was, don't even know it.

Fortunately, God loved me too much to let me stay there. When He began whispering, "Laura, you are a grace killer," I balked. Surely, the devil was trying to distract me. But no, it was God. He was lovingly chastising me.

He knows I love Him. And He wanted me free from the chains, fears, shame, and hard-heartedness of legalism. The freedom is indescribable. It's the abundant life Jesus describes.

Not long ago, I asked my husband what he thought I had done right as a stepmom. He amazed me with this, "You're a great Nana. You show my kids what a good marriage looks like," and "You sacrifice and do things I know you don't want to do."

And that's when I know I'm still becoming a Smart Stepmom.

I close with Isaiah 61. God gave it to me when I started working in divorce recovery during the late 1980s. It's carried me through many years of ministry. I pray it blesses you and your stepfamily.

The Spirit of the Sovereign LORD *is on me,*
because the Lord has anointed me
to proclaim good news to the poor.
He has sent me to bind up the brokenhearted,
to proclaim freedom for the captives
and release from darkness for the prisoners,
to proclaim the year of the Lord's favor
and the day of vengeance of our God,
> *to comfort all who mourn,*
and provide for those who grieve in Zion—
to bestow on them a crown of beauty instead of ashes,
the oil of joy instead of mourning,
and a garment of praise instead of a spirit of despair.
They will be called oaks of righteousness,
a planting of the LORD *for the display of his splendor.*
They will rebuild the ancient ruins
and restore the places long devastated;
> *they will renew the ruined cities*
that have been devastated for generations.
Instead of your shame you will receive a double portion,
and instead of disgrace you will rejoice in
> *your inheritance.* Isaiah 61:1-4, 7

More Resources

For more Laura Petherbridge blended-family resources, visit her at TheSmartStepmom.com, where you can download these easy-to-read ebooks:

- Stepmom Prayers
- Stepmom Steps to Letting Go
- Stepmom Handbook for Mother's Day
- Death in a Stepfamily
- Setting Healthy Boundaries
- Seeking a Silent Night: Unwrapping a Stepfamily Christmas

www.ingramcontent.com/pod-product-compliance
Lightning Source LLC
Chambersburg PA
CBHW032110090426
42743CB00007B/300